REAL LIFE SCHOOL

REAL LIFE SCHOOL

● ● ●

ADULTING 101

Tyler Pencek

**Fundamental Lessons for a Rising Generation
to Succeed in the *Real* World**

ISBN: 1542820812
ISBN 13: 9781542820813
Library of Congress Control Number: 2017901471
CreateSpace Independent Publishing Platform
North Charleston, South Carolina

CONTENTS

ACKNOWLEDGMENTS

THIS IS THE part where I spill the beans on who helped me, how much work people put in to get this book where it is today, and *how I couldn't have done it without you!* Well, it's true! I'm not a writer, and without the names I mention, this book wouldn't be as special as it is. Here it goes: Editor Mike, thanks for putting up with me; Jessica Spinks with Career Cardio, you've been with me since the beginning, and I won't forget any of it; Mom, Dad, Stephie, Rick, Brewhaus, EAL, and Uncle Stan, you guys have been an incredible support base with this project, and thank you for boosting me up when I needed it most. Friends from the S-4 Stackhouse, thanks for letting me teach you some things. Tase Bailey, you will forever be a mentor to me. In this section, someone always gets left out, but it's not intentional. Here are a few more thanks to Smarms, Farva, Benson, Fran, Buscemi, Whimm, Hard Time, Tank, Cream, Woody, Bubbles, Mahu, Mud Rat, Bigsby, Zoltan, Sammy, Michele Lee, Hannah Denise, and many others who listened to me get on my soapbox. You have all been there to help me in some way.

CHAPTER 1

• • •

AN IDEA IS BORN

Too many younger Americans are deficient in monetary, investment, or simple business processes. Our schools have utterly failed the American education system.

—Anonymous

THE CONCEPT BEHIND this book was conceived one morning in December 2007. There was nothing different, nothing special or unique about this morning, and that was part of the problem. It was as if I simply awoke from a dreary haze, shook the sleep away from my eyes, and saw the world around me for the first time.

"What the heck am I doing?!" I asked a lamppost as it zipped by. I was riding my bike in the snow wearing a business suit, on my way to a business presentation (the subject of which escapes me, though it was *obviously* extremely important). Why was I working my ass off to get a degree? I realized that I had not been taught anything of value. Just show up to class, do my homework, and I'd get a degree. I could then use the degree to land a job I hated to pay off my debt and maybe, just maybe, have the resources to chase the things that make me happy after I retire. *What kind of a future is that?*

It seems like this generation and the generations before have been force-fed as kids the idea that we *must get a degree* and that graduation is the insurance policy to success. Meanwhile, my college years taught me absolutely nothing—zilch—about making sustainable money, thinking outside the box, or inventing a life-changing product. Our education system has set a standard, and that standard, to be frank, sucks. Attending college as a business major meant learning how to conform to a corporate structure, as well as learning the "right" way to manage, standardized accounting formats, the hierarchy of the business structure, and countless other cookie-cutter concepts that make me want to break all my fingers just so I don't have to type about them. Nothing I learned in college got me excited about being different, made me want to start a new company, or inspired innovation. I was destined to be a corporate drone trapped in a thankless system, working for years to attain something that I wasn't even sure I wanted, all the while completely oblivious to the details of what it meant to be an adult. I wanted to be passionate about my life. But there was simply no way that the path that I was on, along with all the other lemmings, was ever going to get me there. There needed to be a class on *passion*, *tenacity*, and *dedication*.

It was on this memorable December morning that the concept of "Real Life School" bloomed in my mind. The education system had not taught me how to make (or save) real money, buy a house, buy a car, work credit cards to my advantage, start a company, or be passionate about my next forty working years. I wanted to create something like a Bill Gates or Steve Jobs, not simply because they were wealthy, but because they were innovators who *pursued their passion* and had something to offer the world. They were practical minded and goal driven, and they made products and services that literally billions of human beings very much want. I desperately wanted to emulate that type of success, that sort of influence, and give the public something they needed. So I began to work on a series of educational modules that teach "real-life" topics, things people actually need to know!

Real Life School was established for everyone who has even the slightest idea about the "dos and don'ts" of life, because everyone picks up bits and pieces along the way. We make mistakes that bring us years of financial and personal headaches because there were no classes, no seminars, and no formal instruction whatsoever on how to initiate and successfully complete the real-life actions required in our society (buying a car or house, building credit, investing, etc.). I started off by asking some very fundamental questions: What if we didn't have to learn the hard way? What if someone handed us a book that consolidated the real-life information we needed to be successful and chase our dreams? It sounds like a fantastic, unrealistic concept, because society has told us that happiness takes decades of working our fingers to the bone first. But I don't believe that for a minute.

Breaking news: not all people are born equal! Some get a head start on the ladder of life, but you *can* climb that ladder by understanding the world you are in and learning and applying certain life skills, along with some financial basics, that will help you at each step along the way. Think about where you are now and what you truly want from life. Not everyone desires the same type of success, but there are many people who, once they reach their forties and fifties, regret that they did not make more of their lives. You get to decide, right now, how successful you want to be. Life is full of risks, and Real Life School (RLS) is an insurance policy toward your success.

RLS gives you practical and realistic approaches for helping you achieve that success. First, we need to have a baseline and say something about the history of education in America. We begin with the colonial period, when the idea of higher education was pretty much confined to preaching the Gospel. Back in the early days of America, that was the main objective of such elite institutions as Harvard, Princeton, and Yale. Somehow, we have lost our practical way.

As time went on, and society became more complex and sophisticated, there came the need for arithmetic—good old-fashioned math. This was what people used to sometimes call "ciphering." A farmer, for example, needed to know how much his land yielded in a certain season and what to charge for his produce in the marketplace. He had to know how to make money, give change, and so on—all related to math.

Then, society became even more complex, and things like the Industrial Revolution came into the picture, sparking the need for engineers, scientists, and innovators in many fields. Great strides in this area took place, but they would not have ever occurred were it not for people with specialized skills obtained from education.

Education became the goal of "advanced" societies, and people began thinking about what children "should learn" in school to be successful in the new age. A lot of good came out of teaching literature, poetry, and other academic topics that defined a cultured person. But how practical was all of that for the real world?

At this point, the controversy became "What gives more value, a liberal-arts education or a practical one in business or science?" To some degree, that controversy still rages today, and it helps explain why we have so many problems.

I have learned that, above and beyond these factors, there is no curriculum out there these days to specifically teach you, in depth, many of life's most applicable lessons. Society as always is yearning for knowledge, but not necessarily just in the three basics of education: reading, writing, and arithmetic. People want (and *need*) to know how to be successful in *life*. Among many other things, this includes how to get that job they dream of, how to make that first million bucks, how to make a budget, and how to otherwise take care of themselves. Young men and women must learn all the basic skills that will help them in life's journey. In other words, a wide spectrum of practical life lessons in the broadest sense can have far more value than what you receive from traditional education alone.

Let's face it; in today's society the world revolves around money. Our culture doesn't build things like we used to. *We don't create or build; we work and spend.* What I want to do here is open your eyes. I can't do it for you...you must *want* to do it.

Real Life School is about removing the blindfold from your eyes and seeing the world and what it has to offer you. If you're hell-bent on getting through life alone with no help, put this book down and continue learning from your mistakes. That's the norm anyway. By the way, learning the hard way typically involves a monetary loss of some sort. If, however, you'd like to streamline your education on the real-life topics that haunt the back of your mind so that you can focus on the things you actually find important and pursue your passion, then turn the page, and let's change your life. After you're done with this book, I want you to check out my website (RealLifeSchool.com). The book and website will help you during your journey. Dare to be different!

That is the essence of my effort in this book—to teach you what nobody else has ever bothered to teach you—and in the process, help prepare you for life.

CAREER

CHAPTER 2

• • •

PASSION

WHEN YOU LOOK at your life, you must accept that, as an adult, you have (maybe) seventy years of life to live, and that's *if you're lucky*. Now, we as Americans have access to state-of-the-art health care compared to the rest of the world. We don't see this because we, as a collective group, have not been exposed to other countries where health care is still in its infancy, but just trust me when I say how lucky we are to be here and how little time we have.

This is the best time in the history of humanity to be alive...so don't waste it. We have access to anything and everyone on this planet right at our fingertips. What are we doing with it? Most people hang their heads playing mind-numbing games, or they waste their precious lives trying to build an online image for others to look at and (they hope) admire. We can do things on our cell phones that supercomputers couldn't do twenty years ago, and we can do it instantaneously. We're able to communicate face-to-face across the planet at this very moment. Do we use this amazing technology to improve our lot in life? No. Instead, we tweet; we Facebook; we play wasteful games. Ask yourself, can a monkey do what I'm doing? If so, punch yourself in the face! Come on, people; wake up and realize that *we have a gift*...how stupid we are that we haven't even begun to learn how to use it!

So, what are we going to do about it?

IT'S NOT A JOB ANYMORE!

When you get up before your alarm clock and don't instantly reach over to hit the snooze button, you are well on your way. But first you need to find something to ignite that spark in you. First and foremost, *never pick a career based strictly on money*. Trust me; play the game smart, and the money will come naturally. The top 1 percent of the population make roughly 95 percent of the total income produced. Do you think if you love what you do and you're really good at it, you won't make money? No, the money will come! Find what you are passionate about! The reason the 1 percent of professionals in any field are so successful is that they have found what they *love* to do, and in turn, they are really good at it. Therefore, the money will eventually come around! Follow what you love, follow what you truly excel at, and never do anything just for the money. Otherwise, you will undoubtedly live to regret it. The common denominator for success is *passion*.

> Do what you love and the money will follow.
>
> —Milkman

Some people reading this will find themselves already in a life or career situation that they feel is unacceptable. Let's say you were madly in love and got married young. Suddenly, while still only in your early twenties, you suddenly have a spouse and two kids to support, not to mention that brand-new car (we'll get to this later). You might think that, in your situation, the idea of a career that you love is pure fantasy. You need to work at your unskilled, thankless job just to keep a roof over your family and food on the table. You are probably thinking that I'm talking directly to you as you read this. Good, this should surely hit home with you then.

Stop thinking like that! Situations like those described above do not mean that you can't follow the same plan of thinking and planning for your dream job and a better life. It's not over yet. What kind of team gives up when they haven't even reached halftime yet? And I'm not talking about waiting for your "ship to come in" with a winning lottery ticket, or a rich old neighbor to bequeath you a lot of money in his or her will. No, the important thing is to realize exactly what you want and then make a detailed plan about how you're going to get it. Finally, execute that plan to the best of your ability, and *never give up!* Don't just waste time and wait for your lousy job to one day magically become something exciting; that simply isn't going to happen. You see, you don't even like the field you're in, so your only way out is to find your passion. That is the key. Remember, we only have so much time here. Please don't waste it; please don't tell me you'll get around to it, because frankly...we are not guaranteed tomorrow.

As for the money issue, yes, the world revolves around money. Whether it's the US dollar or the German mark, everyone is "working" to receive some sort of currency or tangible asset to exchange for other goods and services. What I want you to remember is that if you do what you love, the money will follow. Find your passion.

Okay, so now you're asking yourself, how do I find what I truly love? My passion? Some people feel they need to leave their job to follow their passion. However, there are others, of course, who love their current job. Their "job" is already their passion. Which is why, to them, it doesn't feel like a job at all. This situation is just the opposite of the example above. This person already has found his or her passion.

However, there are others still who cannot find happiness either in a full-time job or through self-employment. They search aimlessly trying to find that "passion" in their life. Finding your passion may take time and work, and it will require an equal amount of time and work to keep it burning.

1. WHAT ARE YOU REALLY GOOD AT?

List everything that comes to mind about what you are very good at. I mean, do some real soul-searching and identify what you *truly* are good at—God-given talent! This is the time to be cocky and confident.

Be true to yourself while answering this. Again, this is no time for half-truths, maybes, perhapses, I'll think about it laters, or any other shade of ambivalence. It's time for brutal honesty. Nobody needs to see your list if you're shy or ashamed, but who cares anyway! This is *your* list! Ask others what you are good at, like bosses, coworkers, and close relatives. Sometimes we do not see our own best qualities, which is part of the problem.

2. WHAT DO YOU REALLY LOVE TO DO?

List everything that comes to mind about what you really love to do. This can be anything. I want you to identify whatever it is that makes you happy. Soul-search. This should be the most honest type of evaluation. This is the rest of your life you're dealing with, and it's no time or place to kid yourself. I know you always wanted to be an astronaut, but with zero ability or technical training, forget about that. We're talking reality here. What do you love to do the most? Don't answer this based on someone possibly seeing your list—no need to impress anybody here. This is your confidential talk with yourself. Be open-hearted and real with yourself. Again, it is the time for the real meaning of soul-searching.

3. THE PAYOFF—DREAM JOB OR CAREER.

How can you link the first two lists? It's a simple matter of comparing and contrasting what you like with what you love. Naturally, you'll be happiest if you can accommodate for what you love, so be selfish and don't be ashamed of your braggadocio. The only condition is to make sure it is within the realm of real life. In other words, it should be something that, if you got the chance, you could realistically do with some training.

WHAT DO YOU WANT TO DO? Only you can answer it! Here is an example to see how easy it is....

What do you LOVE to do?	What are you GREAT at?	What type of industry do you see between what you LOVE and what you're GREAT at…? (THAT'S THE INDUSTRY)
• Watch the food channel • Playing Golf • Working Out • Flying • Spending time with family • Listening to music • Traveling to the beach	• Cooking • Starting Conversations with strangers • Hand Eye Coordination • Socializing with new groups • Organizational Skills • Being Creative	• Starting a food business •Possible Pilot •Public Relations Industry

This is just an example:

Watching the Food Channel + Cooking = You could possibly start a food eatery

Flying + Hand Eye Coordination + Good Driving Record = Maybe a Pilot

Spending quality time + Socializing = Possible Public Relations or Marketing Job

You see how you can make the link between the first and second column and draw some conclusions in the third column? Use the blank table I put in the back of the book to write everything down that pertains to you. Remember, the more specific you are, the easier it is to figure out what you want!

Here are some good initial steps to trying to find a passion:

- Find a mentor, and ask as many questions as possible. If they don't want to help, screw 'em!

- Work for free in different fields.
- Be humble.
- "Persistence beats resistance."
- Bridge the gap in your knowledge. Read, research, do your home-work, and continue to learn!

If you get into something that you don't love, doing it just for the money, you will no doubt burn out—and probably sooner rather than later. Chase after what will make you happy, because it has the best possible chance to make you rich.

Very often, you will be passionate about anything that you find impor-tant or that you place value on. Understanding your values and knowing what you find meaningful can help you choose a career or find work you truly enjoy; resolve conflicts with others and within yourself; hire, manage, or mentor others; achieve more personal growth; and decide which direc-tion to go to be who you truly are. So, what do you value? To help identify some value "groups," we'll look at Eduard Spranger's six values or at-titudes that he identified, values that we all possess to varying degrees: theoretical, utilitarian, aesthetic, social, individualistic, and traditional.

Theoretical: If this is your highest value, you have a **passion for knowledge**—knowledge for its own sake. Your ultimate goal is to dis-cover truth, and you believe everything must be rationally justified. You like doing research, reading, studying, and learning. You believe, as Sir Francis Bacon did, that "knowledge is power." If you don't know who this is, look it up on your cell phone that's sitting on your lap or right next to you!

Utilitarian: Your goal is **utility**. You are practical and will maximize your assets. Your passion is a return on investment of your time, talent, or resources. You will enjoy a career in sales or become a CEO or entrepre-neur. You measure your success by how much you have accomplished in a day's work.

Aesthetic: Your goal is to **experience your inner vision**. Your pas-sions are beauty, balance, form, and harmony in all aspects of life. You like for things to run smoothly and may feel more stressed than most others when faced with adversity. You must always be **surrounded by beauty as you define it**. You are profoundly interested in the arts or nature and may choose one as your lifetime career. These career choices probably include the fine arts: acting, painting, drawing, modeling, music, and so on. Each of these skills is something you will need to learn to be good at if you are going to be successful. This may take more self-sacrifice and more dedication than other more achievable, less glamorous professions. Yet if this is what you want, this is what you should aim for. Your goal should be to simply do it and not worry particularly about becoming a huge success at it. After all, not everyone can necessarily win a Grammy or an Oscar, but you can still do your "thing" (whatever that turns out to be), enjoy it, and thrive on it.

Social: This means humanitarian, not sociable. You believe **service to others** is the highest calling in life. You are compassionate and would give your last dime to a homeless person. You must have a career or lifestyle that provides you with opportunities to serve. You're lucky here because there are many opportunities to serve. You may or may not make a lot of money, but what you do make will come easily for you.

Individualistic: You are driven to **use your power and status to achieve your goals and advance your causes**. Your passion is to control your own destiny, as well as the destiny of others. Status and authority are important to you. You will be a captain of industry if your utilitarian value is also high, or you will serve in the military or law enforcement if your social or traditional values are also high. You can prepare yourself for this by getting the right type of education and by making the right social contacts. I still believe it's a "who you know" mentality out there, so cherish those relationships you have that are genuine!

Traditional: Your goal is to **search for and find the highest meaning in life**. Your quest is a system for living. You believe in a higher order of life and consider yourself highly religious or spiritual. You like order and structure, and you need to do meaningful work that rewards quality service. Again, this is an area that you must prepare yourself for with the proper education. The rest will come quite naturally to you.

As we can see, most of us are a combination of at least a couple of these value groups. These values should help lead you to discover optimal career ideas. But no matter the destination, obstacles are sure to get in your way. So, what helps people continue undaunted, staying positive about the future? For some, it is the very presence of a challenge that keeps them going. The list of famous people who were initially discouraged but succeeded beyond anyone's expectations is nearly endless. The most famous example would likely be Albert Einstein, who did not do particularly well in his early days as a student. Sylvester Stallone was homeless, sold his dog, and then made the first *Rocky* movie and soon became a household name. Bill Gates, Oprah Winfrey, Mark Zuckerberg, Stephen Spielberg, Michael Jordan...they all had similar experiences. For these people, ignoring the naysayers was critical to their success. They knew they were in control of their actions and reacted to the world accordingly, realizing that when other people were negative to them, they didn't have to listen. Their success in their respective fields became legendary. One idea that I hold very dear is not allowing anyone tell you that you can't do something! This saying has been talked about throughout history, so just remember, if there is something you want, *anything at all*, just go for it! I will tell you, at the end of the day, you will look back on your life and be completely amazed at what you've accomplished if you just keep fighting through. My grandfather told me, "Laugh in the face of adversity," and you know what? He was right.

For other people, it is the presence of possibilities that sustains their motivation. Instead of looking at the world as a series of challenges to be completed, these positive thinkers see the opportunities in everything, even those that come from hard times. This is the person who sees the loss of a job as the chance to have a new, more satisfying career, or the student who sees a failing grade not as a failure but as a sign that he or she needs better study habits; these people are always thinking posi-tively. When one door closes, another door opens...you don't want to be the one who says, "Well, that was the only door!"

Life is a maze, recognize the signs for opportunity.

—MAMA

Another way of staying positive is by taking risks. Not jumping-out-of-airplanes-without-a-parachute risks, but healthy risks. Doing something you have never done before just for the experience of it has many bene-fits. You should do something that scares you at least once a day. Whether it is getting up in class to speak your mind or talking to that person you have been interested in for a while, just try to conquer your fears. Who cares if it doesn't go the way you wanted? At least you had the moral fortitude to say something and act on it. In other words, you must leave your comfort zone and venture out into the world of possibilities, no mat-ter how "scary" they are. There's a big wide world out there ready for you to explore and enjoy. But it will never happen if you just sit on your butt waiting for something good to come along.

Attitude is contagious. It is harder to stay positive in an environment that is full of grumpy people. You need to keep your head up 24/7 and constantly look at the big picture. It's important to keep up that positive attitude, or you can run into a constant negative environment around you, inevitably decreasing productivity along with communication because people don't want to interact with each other anymore. *This is no good!* Every time you walk into a room, smile—even if it's a fake smile. If people are having a bad day, the smile will show them that you are not someone who wants to fight or argue, but someone who is in a good mood and can't be fazed by negativity.

Finally, positive people can learn how to let go. They know that they can change certain things and work to do just that, but they are realistic enough to acknowledge that other things are outside their control. Let's face it; if you don't have the aptitude for it, you will never be an architect, play a violin, or be president. Remember this prayer: "Lord, grant me the strength to accept things I cannot change, the courage to change the things I can, and the wisdom to know the difference." What a great piece of wisdom. Some things cannot be changed by just one person. Perhaps the positive person can gather other people to help change these things that are broken, but just needs the right team.

So now that we know how to stay positive in difficult times, it's time to get started on developing our passion.

Be willing. The first step is to simply be willing to look beyond all the barriers that you may feel confine you. To look beyond these barriers takes *courage*. Sometimes, we erect those barriers ourselves, out of our own fear of fully living. Are you afraid of what others might think? Who cares! Are you afraid that you won't be financially secure? Who cares! Are you afraid that you might fail? Who cares! These are the sorts of fears that can hold you back. This generation is full of people who are afraid of failure. An old friend of mine and I were talking one day, and he told me how severely disappointed he was by my generation. He used the base-ball analogy of getting up to the plate to hit. He said, "When I was a kid, if I struck out, I didn't want to go back to the bench; I wanted to stay up at the plate and smash the ball. Nowadays, kids may or may not get up to the plate to begin with, and if they do, and they strike out, someone takes a picture or submits something online that makes fun of them, so they head back to the bench and never want to get up to bat again, because they were embarrassed."

My friend nailed it. We are so worried about our image and what others may think of us. My advice is to get up to bat and take a chance. *Who gives a damn* if someone makes fun of you? We are not perfect all the time! It takes time and practice to become good at something. Sometimes you invent these fears just so that you will not have to risk living passionately.

The only thing we have to fear is fear itself.

—Franklin D. Roosevelt

When fear is conquered, it turns to confidence.

—Milkman

Your first step is simply this: be willing to live outside the box you've created with your own fears. Let me tell you something: once fear is conquered, it turns into *confidence*. You'll shoot for the stars once you realize you can accomplish something that has long terrified you. Know yourself and always seek self-improvement. Who are you, really? Are you the role you want to play in society? Are you the work you do? Are you your history, what you have accomplished, or all the mistakes you have made? Are you what other people expect of you? You, the *authentic you*, are of course none of these. You will need to push against these identities to liberate yourself, but they are not you. No one may define who you are. No circumstances, no people, no obligations, no history, no failures, no friends, and no enemies can define you. You are perpetually becoming the unique individual who you were born to be. You may be delayed or sidetracked on that adventure, but nothing can ultimately keep you from it against your will. Choose today to know your inner self—that individual who is unique. Notice what inspires and motivates you—what brings you joy. At the end of the day, the people whom "you're afraid of" don't matter; you must live with yourself, not with those other people.

Follow your *heart*. When you follow your heart, you begin to live life with a purpose and without fear. Courageously follow your heart, and you will feel stronger, every aspect of your life more complete. Your vision of a well-lived life becomes clearer, you become bolder and more confident, and your compassion quickly grows. What you are naturally inclined to do will usually be close to your talent set.

Your passion makes you seek more information about what you do, which typically makes you better at it. The better you are at something, the more confident you become. The more confident you are, the more magnetic you are, and many times that means earning more money, especially in the long run.

Whenever you discover something that interests you, read and research your topic in depth. I can always get myself excited for a subject just by reading about it. Why do you think that is? Most writers are passionate about their subject matter. When they're not, it shows.

Once you have found a topic, develop and enhance your skills in that area. Beyond just reading about the subject, get hands-on with it. Developing your skills in an area will help you develop your passion and enhance your life. Doing more with your life will help you become more enthusiastic about it! Don't be afraid of failure; test yourself. That's how you become self-taught, and remember, you can always improve on your mistakes.

Ask, "What if?" That's what a fiction writer constantly does. He or she imagines a scenario where people get involved in certain unique and interesting situations. This is the fuel to make a novel take off and capture the reader's attention. Apply the same concept to your passion. Once you've become knowledgeable and have acquired a certain level of skill, challenge the currently accepted theories in the subject area. New inventions are created this way.

Share your passion—teach others. You don't really know something until you have to teach it to someone. Teaching is also selling. When you need to stand in front of people and sell them something, you'd better be passionate about it. Just talking about your subject can ignite that little spark you need to take your passion to the next level.

Develop your passion by surrounding yourself with others who already share your thoughts and beliefs. Professional organizations quite often fill the bill nicely here. Not only are the other participants "freaks" about the topic, but these associations offer additional educational opportunities and a chance to develop useful skills as well.

Overall, why do you want to waste your life doing something you do not enjoy? Ask yourself these questions and answer them *sooner* rather than later! Remember, you only have so much time here on Earth, so what are you going to do about it?

> I do things now that most people don't want to do, so
> later in life I can do things that most people can't do!
>
> —BREWHAUS

CHAPTER 3

• • •

JOB APPLICATIONS AND INTERVIEWS

IT IS COMMON, of course, to have some anxiety when it comes to landing a job. Naturally, you feel that a big part of your future is at stake. As with most things, even a small amount of preparation will take you a long way. *Some* questions to ponder (and answer!) before you appear for your interview are as follows:

- What goods and/or services do they provide? Do your research and know what type of company they are. Do they have many employees or just a few?
- What types of responsibilities are there? Are there certain things you should know or skills you should have if you wish to work there? If you know people who currently work there, ask them how they like it.
- What are the expectations? Is this a full-time or a part-time job? Is the schedule flexible, and will it fit your other responsibilities?
- Know the requirements. For example, what does it take to get that particular job? What are the minimum qualification requirements, or sex and age requirements (discrimination is not allowed, but these requirements are still a reality)?
- Know the location of that job. Is the environment favorable?
- Know about the salary scale or wage. Is the salary favorable in relation to your lifestyle, experience, and qualifications?
- Know about the management. Is the management well organized? Is the company profitable?

- Consider the benefits. Are they offering benefits like medical? Do they pay for educational courses for job-skill improvement?
- Get advice from experienced personnel regarding the job. Take note of the closing date for applications.
- The interview is usually the final step in determining whether or not you get the job, except perhaps for the follow-up that is sometimes necessary. Some companies even require several interviews during their screening process.

APPLYING FOR A JOB

Of course, before you get any type of job (it doesn't matter what you'll be doing), you must apply to the company. This is going to take effort on your part to prove that you are the candidate whom they desperately *want* to meet.

The most important rule to remember when applying for jobs is to follow the directions they give you. If the employer tells you to apply in person, don't call. If the job posting says to mail your résumé, do not send it via e-mail. When the job listing says to apply via a form on the company website, don't e-mail your application directly to human resources. But even if you submit a résumé to a company, once you go for the interview, you will also be asked to complete a job application. This way the employer will have consistent data on file for all prospective applicants. Also, your signature on the job application acknowledges that the information is accurate to the best of your knowledge. There are rules and standards...even if some of them seem completely ridiculous or a dumb and wasteful way of doing things, follow them to the letter. Honestly, my take is that if you want the work bad enough, you'll do whatever it takes to get the job!

Remember to always bring the information you'll need to fill out an application with you. This should be your full contact information, including your address, your zip code, and a phone number where you can be reached. Educational information you provide should include any dates of graduation. In fact, have all important and relevant dates handy. Next come references: the names and addresses of previous employers. If you have one, carrying a résumé is always professional. Also, bring a pen so you don't need to borrow one to fill out the application (*make it a habit: don't ever be caught without a pen!*).

Know what days and hours you are available to work. If you're applying for a job, you will work whenever they need you! Be prepared for a brief, on-the-spot interview, and dress appropriately. Research should always be your first step. That old "Be Prepared" Boy Scouts motto is really good advice here. Gathering background information on employers is a crucial element in successful interview preparation. You will need to be prepared to answer the questions "What do you know about our company?" and "Why do you want to work here?" Knowing as much as possible about the company's past performance and future plans can make your interview more interactive and could be just the leg up you need in a competitive job market. This will also show the interviewer that you have invested time in researching the company. Before the interview, review the company's website, and don't be afraid to contact your prospective employer to request details on the position you are interviewing for or to ask for company literature. Google the company to see what other information is available to you online.

MAKING A GOOD IMPRESSION AT AN INTERVIEW

Of course, you want to make the best impression you possibly can. The following are some tips you can use to make sure that you do just that.

Appearance: Appearance makes a powerful first impression. It is a key part of planning for your interview. Dress appropriately. Remove any body piercings and cover all visible tattoos. Take all necessary documentation with you in a neat portfolio cover. Bring an extra copy of your résumé and a list of references. There is no right answer as to what you should wear, but you need to do some homework on the type of company you're applying to. A suit for both men and women can be appropriate for some job interviews, but maybe slacks and collared shirt or a skirt may be appropriate for another interview. *Use good judgment.* It is always better to be overdressed than to be underdressed.

Below are guidelines for men and women on what they should consider wearing to an interview. If you need more information or want some great advice on how to land that dream job, contact Jessica Spinks at CareerCardio.com.

INTERVIEW STYLE GUIDE FOR MEN:

- Suit: A traditional suit is most standard. Wear it with a collared shirt underneath. A tie is optional depending on the circumstances.
- Color: Black, blue, or gray. Don't detour from this.
- Shoes: Clean and shiny shoes in black or brown are always good.
- Accessories: Cufflinks and minimal jewelry are key here. Go light on the cologne. Take out all piercings.
- Briefcase or folder: Your résumé should be inside one of these, never in a backpack. A briefcase is a good option that helps you appear more professional.

INTERVIEW STYLE GUIDE FOR WOMEN:

- Suit: A two-piece skirt-suit is most standard and is the best choice. Wear it with a silk or collared blouse underneath. Make sure your outfit is well ironed and your undershirt is clean and well pressed.
- Color: Black, gray, or dark blue are standard, but don't be afraid to have fun. Show your personality; just ensure that your clothes are not the only thing they remember about you.
- Shoes: Heels are traditional, in black or a neutral color. Make sure your shoes are clean and in good shape.

- Accessories: Keep accessories to a minimum, but also don't be shy to show some personality. Don't overdo it with the perfume! Take out all piercings aside from earrings if it is a very professional working environment. In addition, no undergarments should be showing. A neutral bra is important.
- Bag, briefcase, or folder: Your résumé should be inside one of these, never in a bulky purse or a backpack. Your bag should act as a supporting role.

If you need more help or advice, like I said, contact Career Cardio for more info. They will suggest that you dress one step above the environment you will be going into.

Time: It is very important to be on time for the interview. Hint: on time means ten to fifteen minutes *early*. If need be, take some time to drive to the office ahead of time so you know exactly where you are going. You'll feel more relaxed that way, too.

Show Respect: During the interview, be tactful, courteous, sincere, polite, and knowledgeable about the organization and what you have to offer them. The idea here is to leave them with a lasting impression that you would make a good fit as a member of their team. Also, know the interviewer's name, and use it often (but not too often) during the interview. This will demonstrate that you are a personable team player.

Practice beforehand: Practice makes perfect (or at least leads to improvement). Practice with a friend and record your responses so you can replay the interview and see how well you did with it. It is especially important to prepare answers to commonly asked interview questions. Doing so will help you analyze your professional background and qualifications for the position. Let's examine some of these common questions they may ask you.

Traditional interview questions:

- What are your strengths and weaknesses?
- What major challenges and problems did you face?
- How did you handle them?
- Describe a typical workweek.

Be sure not to use trendy, overused, and outright corny responses to questions about your work ethic, such as "My main fault is I work too hard at my job" or other lame clichés.

In a behavioral interview, an employer has already decided what skills are needed in the person they wish to hire and will ask questions to find out if the candidate has those skills. Instead of asking how you *would* behave, they will ask how you *did* behave. The interviewer will want to know how you handled a situation, instead of what you might do in the future. So have this in mind and prepare your response. If you are familiar with your story, you won't falter when you're relaying it in the interview.

Behavior-based interviewing is becoming more common than traditional processes. It is based on the premise that a candidate's past performance is the best predictor of future performance. Rather than the typical interview questions on your background and experience, you will need to be prepared to provide detailed responses, including specific examples from your prior work experiences.

The best way to prepare is to think of examples where you have successfully used the skills you've acquired over the years. Take the time to compile a list of responses to both traditional and behavioral questions and to itemize your skills, values, and interests as well as your strengths and weaknesses. Behavioral interview questions will be more pointed, more probing, and more specific than traditional interview questions. For instance:

- Give an example of an occasion when you used logic to solve a problem.
- Give an example of a goal you reached and tell me how you achieved it.

- Describe a decision you made that was unpopular and how you handled implementing it.
- Have you gone above and beyond the call of duty? If so, how?
- What do you do when your schedule is interrupted? Give an example of how you handled it.
- Have you had to convince a team to work together on a project they weren't thrilled about? How did you do it?
- Have you handled a difficult situation with a coworker? How?
- Tell me about how you've worked effectively under pressure.

With all these questions, emphasize what you can do to benefit the company rather than just what you are interested in. Also, prepare a list of questions you want to ask the interviewer. Such as:

- What will my day-to-day responsibilities look like?
- How long have you worked here?
- In your opinion, is this really a great company to work for?
- How does the lifestyle of the company affect your personal life?

Remember, you aren't simply trying to get the job—you are also interviewing the employer to assess whether this company and position are a good fit for you. That will become obvious if you use the correct line of questioning. The trick is to not make your questions sound like you are simply trying to get a list of perks and benefits associated with this job and company. Your main purpose should be to ensure that the interviewer knows your goal is to learn about the company and how you would be a great match for it.

Follow the rules: Before you do any of the above, there are a few rules of etiquette to follow.

- Always greet the interviewer and offer a firm handshake.
- Listen carefully for the interviewer's name and title, if you don't already know them (then use them as needed during the rest of the interview).

- Make and maintain eye contact with him or her.
- Be friendly, but not too casual.
- Speak in complete sentences, and use a formal vocabulary.
- Don't fidget, chew gum, smoke, or use slang during your interview.
- Be honest with your responses. You do not have to offer negative information, but be sure you don't lie if asked directly.

Be clear: During the interview, answer clearly and completely with enough information. Take a moment to think before you respond to difficult questions. Organize your thoughts so that you don't ramble. Remain calm, no matter what question is asked of you. You can ask the interviewer to rephrase a question that you are not sure of.

Finish strong: Finally, when the time comes, conclude the interview. Thank the interviewer for the time he or she spent with you. Ask when a decision will be made, if that hasn't already been indicated. Be sure to make notes as soon as you leave. Jot down the name of the interviewer, questions you answered well, questions you could have answered more effectively, and questions you would like to have asked (but didn't). Keep a file of these notes from your interviews that you can use to prepare for the next time.

Follow up: Send a follow-up or a thank-you letter. Type it on good quality paper, or write it by hand. Don't think you can skip it—interviewers *expect* it. Express your thanks for the interview and restate your interest in the opportunity. You can even answer (or ask!) a question you may have missed during the interview.

You can also follow up with a phone call in a week or two to check on the status of your application. Even when you don't land a job after an interview, never view it as a waste of your time. On the contrary, it was a valuable learning experience that will help you keep moving along the road to success.

FINANCES

CHAPTER 4

• • •

CREDIT

ONE OF THE best real-life lessons you can ever learn is this: "If you don't have cash, you can't afford it" (Roger Pencek, aka Pops).

However, don't think that this makes credit a bad thing in and of itself. You just don't want to be stupid with it and get in over your head. Credit has a place in your life, and you will soon understand the importance of how to use it. The fact is that the only way to establish credit is to start buying with credit. Understand that if your credit is flawed, you will be forced to pay more *for the same products and services* than those with good credit, due to interest payments. You're going to spend the money anyway, so why not take advantage of the benefits?

Sometimes it is best to use cash to make purchases, because you can typically get a better deal on items that are not retail but sold between people. For example, paying cash for a used car will most likely get that vehicle for a cheaper price than using credit. Cash on the downside leaves no record of your payment and doesn't show your ability to pay. So you need to establish credit. Let's look at credit and get a handle on how to make yours better.

Three companies (credit bureaus) evaluate your credit score:

- Equifax
- Experian
- Trans Union

In the eyes of these credit-reporting bureaus, you are a portfolio, résumé, or account that these companies hold on file.

Your credit score is your "grade" that determines how risky you are as a prospective borrower. If you're too risky, or you don't have a good "credit résumé," then your interest rates on the money you borrow will increase. *Your credit is your interview.*

WAYS TO BUILD CREDIT

- Open a checking or savings account (parents can open one up for their kids in their name). Without a checking or savings account, the reporting service has no way of knowing what you have or what your saving record is like. In fact, without either account you're not even a financial entity to the outside world.
- Open a credit card. Parents can open a "mutual credit card" using their child's name. This is yet another way to track your payment record and the way you handle your responsibilities.
- Take out a car loan (used or new). This, of course, is a form of credit and an excellent way to see how well you pay back money and establish a credit record for yourself.
- Open a line of credit. This is what the companies you are dealing with think you are capable of handling financially, based on your income and paying habits.
- Keep a job. It used to be that people worked at one big American company until retirement, and they received a gold watch. That's great for credit. But people are more mobile today, changing jobs and moving around the country. That used to be considered unstable and was undesirable. Today, it is not. So long as you have a record of *steady employment*, you will be good for obtaining credit.
- Pay your bills on time. If you don't pay bills on time, simply because it's not a high priority to you, think again. A record

of paying utilities, rent, and other bills on time bodes well for getting credit.

- Rent an apartment. This is another way for a potential creditor to see how you handle your obligations. This is true whether you're sloppy with payments or you're scrupulous with your payments. If you are habitually late, this will be a bad sign for any company considering your creditworthiness. If you are always on time, you're well on your way to achieving good credit.

GOOD DEBT VERSUS BAD DEBT

A home mortgage and a credit card are both good because you are using someone else's money to show the credit companies that you can repay your debt. But one is a matter of keeping a roof over your head, and the other is a matter of satisfying your wants.

The home mortgage is something tangible that increases in value over time (they are not making any more land), paying down principal toward your home.

"Wants" purchased on a credit card could set you back years due to the high interest rates if the debt goes unpaid. Do not keep a running credit-card balance outstanding!

> The poor long for riches, the rich long for wisdom, but the wise long for tranquility.
>
> —RAMA SWAMI

> Live within your means even if you have to borrow money to do so.
>
> —ROBIN WILLIAMS

CREDIT CARDS

If you're going to spend the money anyway, why don't you take advantage of the benefits associated with a card of your choosing? Since it is a very competitive credit-card market, all kinds of incentives are offered to you, the consumer. Airlines offer free miles, consumer credit cards offer special deals, and so on. If you use your Sears credit card to buy a chainsaw, you get a special discount. Some give discounts and kickbacks. Others, like Capital One and other major banks, take this one step further and compete on how many discounts and kickbacks ("points") you can get by using their particular card.

> A bank is a place that will lend you money if you prove
> you don't need it.
>
> —BOB HOPE

> A bank will lend you an umbrella and ask for it back when
> it rains.
>
> —ROBERT FROST

Using a card responsibly also builds credit so you can make purchases later that you may not have enough cash for. One other good reason for having credit cards: saving time and energy on unnecessary stress. Let's say you have a medical emergency, your car drops the transmission, or the roof over your house starts to leak. Having a credit card with a high enough limit can bail you out of some of life's most stressing financial problems. So let's go through the steps of using a credit card successfully.

1. SELECT A CARD.

Check for the annual fee. Educate yourself on the benefits of the card and decide whether this annual cost is worth it to you. Many banks offer a student credit card at no expense each year. Many other credit-card companies will promote giving away miles after you spend a certain amount of money. Other companies offer no fees for a year. There are many marketing options that credit-card companies promote to gain your business.

Point system: choose one that you'll not only use, but also benefit from collecting the points. For example, you could get an airline credit card from American Airlines, Southwest, or Delta if you travel a lot, or a Marriott credit card if you frequently stay at hotels. You're going to stay there anyway and pay for it; why don't you take advantage of the points? Bingo!

Perks of the card: with American Express Platinum, you receive $200 a year for expenses on an airline of your choosing, including baggage or alcoholic beverages.

2. KNOW YOUR LIMIT.

Treat the credit card like it's a debit card! We all have heard of people who are in crisis with severe credit-card debt. What has happened in those situations is that they have used their credit cards to the limit without thinking of how to pay it back. *Their debt is not in proportion to their income or ability to pay it back.* This happens all the time. That's why I advise you to know your limit and respect it.

> I haven't reported my stolen credit card to the police.
> Whoever has it is spending less than my wife.
>
> —Anonymous

3. PAY YOUR MINIMUM MONTHLY PAYMENT *AT THE VERY LEAST.*

Ideally, pay your entire bill every month. Some people say to carry a balance of some sort. At least make sure you *pay your minimum*, but know that interest will *kill you!* Annual percentage rate (APR) is what interest you will pay on the outstanding balance (usually16–22 percent). The company must inform you within forty-five days if they are going to change the APR, and usually this is printed on the bottom of your bill that you somehow always *forget* to review. Be warned.

HOW TO GET A CREDIT CARD

Now that we know what to look for, it's time to obtain our card. You must be at least eighteen years of age and be employed or a student. Credit-card companies think so highly of graduates that most companies offer a card with no record, simply for graduating!

There are lots of ways to apply for a credit card:

- Walk into a bank and apply (though it may seem obvious, it will not be to some).
- Have a checking or savings account. That will help you by showing you are financially responsible. Sound obvious? There are scores of people who screw up their checking accounts to the point that a bank will no longer carry them. They overdraw constantly and run negative balances. They are more trouble to the bank than they are worth and are consequently dropped.
- Google any credit-card company and research which one would fit your needs. Do your due diligence and research Visa, American Express, Discover, and MasterCard.
- Get referrals from friends (typically they will also get points for referring you).

MORE THINGS TO THINK ABOUT:

- Never carry a 30–50 percent balance on your card just because some nerd told you that is the best way to build credit. This is just a great way to establish a bad habit of not paying off your bills.

- Always pay on time. Thirty days of not paying will affect your credit.
- Learn the concept of compound interest. Even a relatively small credit-card balance can quickly balloon into a constantly growing debt. Let the table below (based on a 20 percent interest rate on a $1,000 balance over twelve months) serve as a warning...and keep you from creating a huge mess for yourself!

Month	Monthly Interest	Total Interest	Balance
1	$16.67	$16.67	$1,016.67
2	$16.94	$33.61	$1,033.61
3	$17.23	$50.84	$1,050.84
4	$17.51	$68.35	$1,068.35
5	$17.81	$86.16	$1,086.16
6	$18.10	$104.26	$1,104.26
7	$18.40	$122.66	$1,122.66
8	$18.71	$141.38	$1,141.38
9	$19.02	$160.40	$1,160.40
10	$19.34	$179.74	$1,179.74
11	$19.66	$199.40	$1,199.40
12	$19.99	$219.39	$1,219.39

- Look at your statements to be sure all billings are correct. In the age of the Internet, it is an easy matter to commit to some plan or service without understanding what exactly you are committing to. Check your account each month and be sure there are no unauthorized charges. Also, we live in the age of identity theft. You need to make sure that nobody is using your credit card without your knowledge!

BOTTOM LINE:

- If you don't have cash, you can't afford it, at least according to my pops, but if you're going to spend the money, you might as well get the points. Make your money work for you!
- Your balance should be paid in full every month.

CHAPTER 5

• • •

BUYING A CAR

SO MANY PEOPLE today completely misunderstand the purpose of having a vehicle. We go into debt to buy things we don't need, to impress people who don't care about us. During the early stages of our lives, we need to be careful how we spend money, because any little mistake will take more time to correct. It's easier to get out of a bad car situation when you are forty years old and have $100K in the bank than when you are twenty-five years old, making $30K a year, and still living with your parents. A mistake can be relatively costlier at a younger age, when you are not making very much money but just trying to get on your feet.

In the modern world, unless you live someplace where you can truly depend on public transportation, a reliable vehicle is an essential part of everyday life. Of course, if you're not smart about it, that set of wheels can drive you straight to the poorhouse. So many people either have bought or will buy brand-new cars in the future, regardless of how financially successful they are. *Bad move!* We need to take the time to truly assess the reasons why we are buying these cars.

There's one thing I want you to remember: *if you don't have cash, you can't afford it.* End of story. Forget financing. That's just a fancy way of saying you want to buy things that you can't afford. My father instilled this lesson in me as a young kid when I wanted to buy something like a new dirt bike. He asked if I had enough money to buy it and made me look at my bank account. Of course, I didn't. The new, flashy, out-of-my-price-range dirt bike was the one I wanted, but I didn't think about the actual value of the dollar at ten years old. My pops said, "You'd better get out there and sell some more golf balls!" Because we lived on a golf course, I sold golf balls. This was my equivalent of a lemonade stand in which kids try to make a couple bucks during the summer. As I got older and saw even better things that I wanted to buy, I would ask for whatever the item was, and the response was always the same. "You know what you have to do." He was implying that I should get outside and sell some golf balls. This lesson has carried with me throughout my entire life. I think you should learn from it. You know what you need to do.

When car shopping, most people will look for something well beyond their realistic budget range and set themselves up for a $300–$500 per month car payment. This is the typical first step down the wrong road toward becoming financially anchored to *one purchase*. No wonder buying a car is so stressful for most people…

Of course, you want to purchase something that is reliable, safe, and going to last. Well, those are good criteria to follow, but most people also buy cars because it is something they *want*. People will typically buy vehicles based on emotion, status, or external image! This generation thinks that others are always watching us and care so much about us. We therefore believe that they will judge us based on the type of car we drive. *Nonsense!* Honestly, people don't care what you drive, and if they do, you and your car are forgotten about by the next stop-and-go light. So if you spend more than two hours a day in your car, you probably want something comfortable, fuel-efficient, and with low maintenance costs. But don't think that others will judge you based on your car.

Unfortunately, people do not look at the major cost of a depreciating asset when they need to make payments on it. Everyone who is reading this book should know by now that as soon as you have driven that nice, new vehicle off the lot, you cannot (typically) turn around and sell it for more money. In fact, the exact opposite is true, as its value immediately begins to steadily decline. This is the concept of a depreciating asset! Now, you put interest and high payments every month into this car. For some, this works out because they can write off the interest as a business expense. But for the average person who simply needs a vehicle to get from point A to point B, a new car is not the way to go. Not only does it begin to depreciate, but now you're putting gas, tires, oil, and other money for upkeep into this car, which you will not be able to recoup.

I always say, "If you don't have cash, you can't afford it," but this isn't realistic for most people. So, taking a small loan out to purchase a used car may not be a horrible idea, but you need to consider a vehicle as a means of transportation from A to B until you have established yourself and can buy an awesome new vehicle using cash. One of the advantages of buying used cars is less depreciation, meaning you will not lose as much money on the car because it has already been "driven off the lot." You also pay less insurance because they are less expensive to begin with, a double win!

The problem, as it turns out, is that it is easier to buy a $20,000 car at a dealership than it is to by a $3,000 car from a private owner. This is because the dealership is more than prepared to finance you. Even if your credit isn't so hot, you can still get that fancy car. What I mean is, the dealership is the bank. They have in-house money. They approve you with money they have already and just charge you a higher interest rate than a regular bank or credit union would. Of course, poor credit will cost you a lot more in interest…a hell of a lot more! But they suck you in because you don't have to go to a bank or your credit union to fill out paperwork and provide bank statements. The dealer makes it hard to walk away. You can drive out of the dealership in a new car the same day that you pick it out. Sometimes, the dealer can have you banked and out on the road in your brand-new car in an hour or less. But at the end of a couple of years, you will be significantly ahead by going with a used car. Just be sure to follow some general strategies and guidelines.

BUYING A CAR

Always set a maximum amount of money you are willing to spend on a vehicle. Determine what you'll need the car for and for how long you will use it. The time will determine if you should buy an older car (less time you'll keep it) or a newer car (you'll hold on to it longer). Do not buy a vehicle out of fear of judgment. You must set status aside. People do not care about what you are driving as much as they *will* remember that you had a new car and are now begging for money because you went bankrupt. Don't let your misconception of others get in the way of making the mature decision based on your circumstance.

BE SMART

Cars do not last forever; they do not make you money, and nobody cares what you're driving. As you can see, this is another area of life where ego does *not* serve you well. We have just mentioned that people buy cars for impractical reasons. Most of the time, they simply *want* it. They don't *need* it. We make emotional decisions and then find things that justify how we feel. If you feel yourself falling instantly in love with a car, beware! It might be good to force yourself to walk away from the dealership for a bit and let your emotional side battle it out with your logical side. Many people (whether they can afford it or not) choose a car based on the perceived status it gives them. Let's face it; it's a trap, but an effective one for the auto seller. Who doesn't "ooh and ahh" over expensive, late-model luxury cars? Certain high-end brands—Porsche, Mercedes, and Ferrari to name a few—conjure up images of glamor, style, and success. If nothing else, you should learn, if you haven't already, that success is measured in many other ways than that.

So use some common sense when making this purchase. Think about why you need the vehicle. Set a price limit and stick to it. Make sure you do your research on reliability and associated costs so you can make an educated decision on what vehicle you can afford to buy. The Internet has given everyone instant access to any type of information you can possibly think of, so use it!

> People are working jobs they don't like, to buy things
> they don't need, to impress people who don't care.
>
> —Dave Ramsey

> If you think nobody cares if you're alive, try to miss a
> couple of car payments...
>
> —Earl Wilson

THINGS TO THINK ABOUT WHEN BUYING A CAR

- Can I pay cash? Always a preferable option.
- Financing? How does good credit get a good rate? Let's face it. To get the low rate being advertised, you need good credit. This is where it comes in handy.
- New or used? Values of new cars drop immediately. If you drive your new car off the lot and return the next day to trade it in, it will have decreased in value. Sound unfair? Maybe. But it's true.
- Warranty? With the enormous cost of auto repairs today, this is a most important consideration. The longer and more complete a warranty, the better. Think about it. We live in the day where a moon-roof motor costs $1500. Labor costs are way up there too—around $100 per hour, making even the simplest of repairs costly.
- Remember that *you* are the buyer! It is what *you* want that matters most!
- Think about the associated gas, insurance, and maintenance costs, as well as implications of your driving record. When you buy a car, the cost of the vehicle is only the beginning. Then you need local and state excise taxes, insurance, maintenance, gasoline, and parking. The main question should always remain: can I honestly afford all of this?
- How much money will you owe? Let's say you pay the minimum amount of money for a down payment, you stretch the payments out for seventy-two months (common practice nowadays), and you drive a lot of miles. It is likely that in the future, your car will

be worth less than the balance you originally owed the bank or finance company. In this case, you are considered upside down on the car, and when you go to sell or trade, you are going to lose money.

- Check the car's history with outside resources (e.g., Car Fax). There are Internet sites today that can check a lot of things about a car's history, including any accidents it may have been involved in. This is an excellent resource, as you want to stay away from any vehicle that had been involved in a major accident. Many times, after the accident the car will eventually exhibit numerous problems, from mufflers to alignments.

STEPS TO BUYING A CAR

1. Research the vehicle type (including all expenses that are associated with it) for:
   - Safety.
   - Cost (maintenance, tune-ups, gas, tires).
   - Reliability.
   - Insurance.
2. Look up financing options (How are you going to pay for this? *Do not overextend yourself!*)
   - Cash.
   - Loan.
   - Dealer financing—in-house for a new car. It's very easy, but with higher interest rates. You may owe more in the long run.
   - Bank financing—credit plays into this now. There's lots of paperwork involved to obtain proper financing.
3. Search for the car
   - Online (Craigslist, Auto Trader, or any car website)—make sure to ask the seller *all* the appropriate questions!

- Newspaper (yes, they still exist, and you can potentially get great deals)—again, make sure you are asking the relevant questions and aren't getting scammed!
- Drive to the dealership. This one warrants some special explanation. You will be talking to a salesperson who has been trained to make you feel comfortable and put you into a car as soon as possible, hopefully that day. They have a way of talking ragtime about the numbers involved. They'll talk about special deals, discounts, what your trade-in is worth, and so on. The bottom line is this: if you are trading in a car, you are thinking about the car's *retail* price, and they are committed to giving you only the *wholesale* price. Why? They will need to resell your car, and there are costs involved, so the most you are going to get for that car is its wholesale worth. So if you have the time and energy and resources, you are far better off selling it yourself, which is especially difficult to do if the car is fairly new and worth a good price. Few people are sitting around with the thousands needed to buy your car. That's why it's so easy to let the dealership handle it. But, of course, that service comes with a price. Again, you're thinking retail, and they're thinking wholesale.
- New versus old (depreciation, warranty issues, history of the vehicle and the previous driver)
4. Negotiate the deal
   - Check KBB (Kelly Blue Book: national average of vehicles dating back to 1985). This will let you know roughly how much you can expect to spend on a car.
   - Use comparable numbers (from your online research, dealerships, or paper).
   - You now know the market value for this type, model, and series.

Now that you've been given an idea about how to choose the right car for *you*, let me try to summarize with a chart:

New Cars	Used Cars
Pros	Pros
• Reliable • Easy to finance • Have a warranty • Often convey status	• Less expensive • Won't lose as much value • Leave money to invest in other places
Cons	Cons
• More expensive • Can result in buyer's remorse • Value depreciates	• Possibly have no warranty • Uncertain history • Harder to finance

Saving up to buy a car with cash always makes the most economic sense. Over the years, you will save thousands of dollars in interest. If you do finance the purchase, at least make sure that you secure a fixed interest rate and for a short term. Always remember that the longer you still owe existing principal on that vehicle, you will continue to pay interest on that principal month after month, year after year. Start thinking of that (right now!) as money out the window, and you will quickly appreciate the wisdom of either a cash purchase or a short-term, fixed-rate loan. In fact, if you can pay the loan off early without a prepayment penalty, do so. You will thank yourself in the long run.

As we can see, buying a car can be either a great investment or a huge financial burden. Choose wisely, consider all options, and *be smart!*

CHAPTER 6

• • •

REAL ESTATE

REMEMBER THIS: Everyone needs a place to live. Buying real estate can lead to a very prosperous future, but don't leverage your entire income to pay for a house. Be a buyer who is educated, realistic, and setting yourself up for success years down the road.

Four walls and a roof over your head are not just a survival necessity, but where you live exerts a major impact on your life—and on your wallet. In fact, for most people, home ownership represents the biggest invest- ment they will *ever* make. Ask yourself where you want and need to live. This is your homework stage of buying a home.

I will first give you a rough overview of some criteria that should be met when buying a home. Then, I will give you the steps on how to go about actually *doing* it.

LOCATION: DO YOUR HOMEWORK!

You want to live somewhere that is convenient for you in many, if not all, aspects of your life. What I mean is that if you like to eat out often, you should probably live somewhere you would have plenty of options to walk from your home and eat. If you love the outdoors, you need to identify what type of activities you enjoy most and pick a location where you can do those activities without having to make major sacrifices to enjoy that aspect of your life. If you're young, you may want to live close to a location that has the night life you want to enjoy. I personally like to learn about what is going to be built around the city in years to come. I look for a lo- cation where I can purchase for a decent price, and I let the development come to fruition while watching my property value increase. These are some other things to consider when considering a location. Talking with a great friend of mine, both he and I agreed you must be able to answer yes to two of the following three questions to make life enjoyable: Do you like where you live? Do you like what you do? Do you like who you work with? If you hit two of these three, you're set. Just remember that *location* is the key to buying real estate.

WORK COMMUTE

This is no small consideration. Some people have easy commutes, which certainly makes life less stressful (always a good thing). On the other hand, I've heard of people who have horrendous commutes of up to two hours each way. Time is money, and even if you have clocked out of work and you're driving home, you still need to put a price on the value of your own personal time.

So this is not just a matter of convenience. Of course, a twenty-minute ride is easier than a two-and-a-half-hour ride to work, but the important thing here is your health. In time and stress alone, you are getting behind in the effort to lead a happy, healthy life. So I put everything into perspective. If you can buy a house that costs you a hundred dollars a month more, consider that hundred dollars compared to the cost of a four-hour round-trip commute. A long commute is expensive, not to mention the stress and aggravation hit on your general well-being. It can be a hard choice. Let's say you can buy a seaside home with the joy of stress-free, oceanfront living, gazing out at the sea in peace and tranquility. But to get it, you need to take a job that is the commute from hell in terms of distance, traffic, and weather conditions. There's a smarter choice here. Guess which it is? What I want you to take out of this discussion is real perspective on the amount of time, the amount of your *finite life*, you are sitting in your car. Is it really worth buying that cheaper house outside of town if you have to endure an hour-and-a-half commute? This is your life, and your time is precious. *What are you going to do with it?*

NEIGHBORHOOD AND COMMUNITY

The neighborhood you live in should be one in which you want to have yourself and your family living in. This is more important than you might think. Thinking long term includes researching not only whether the neighborhood is tied to good or not-so-good schools, but also its overall quality of life, which is very important. We all know of the pitfalls of living in a crime-ridden neighborhood. Where you live, unfortunately, can also have a bearing on your business and social life. I know people who are not very smart who live in upscale neighborhoods and (simply because of their address, believe it or not) progress faster than those in not-so-desirable locations. Think about it. If you're dealing with somebody from an affluent, upscale community, you feel he or she is more important than someone from a run-down part of town. And usually you would be right.

Here are some practical suggestions about how to go about buying a home:

- Analyze where you are financially and career-wise: identify what your finances look like, what type of income you're currently making, how much debt you have, whether you plan on changing jobs, or whether your job is thinking about moving you. These things all need to be addressed while considering real-estate purchases.
- Set up financing: you need to find the right mortgage company to handle your home purchase. This can be a very stressful process, and you want someone who will be flexible with you while trying to get all the documents and papers signed. They will review your credit records and run a bunch of numbers to make sure your debt-to-income ratio is in line and will then preapprove you for a given amount of money you can spend on a home. This preapproval value is what you are capable of spending on a home. This doesn't mean you should spend that entire value! This is just the maximum amount that you are *capable* of purchasing. Just because you are qualified to purchase a $500K home doesn't mean that you should

only be looking at $500K homes. Maybe you find one that is $350K and now have some breathing room and don't have to max out your lending potential. Your lender should also talk you through the different loan types. There are so many out there, so make sure your lender is educating you about all your options! If you don't know something or have a question, then by all means ask it.

- Obtain your credit check and preapproval for the loan (go to different loan companies and have *them* compete for your business).
- Loan types: below is a table that shows a purchase price of $200K and the difference between putting zero money down, 3.5 percent money down, and 20 percent money down. I have also included the difference in monthly payment between having a thirty-year mortgage and having a fifteen-year mortgage. What I want you to take away is the difference in your monthly payment based on how much money you put down.

Down Payment	Interest Rate	Monthly Payment (30-Year Mortgage)	Monthly Payment (15-Year Mortgage)
No money down	5%	$1,073.64	$1,581.59
$7,000 (3.5%)	5%	$1,036.07	$1,526.23
$40,000 (20%)	5%	$858.91	$1,265.27

The monthly payments do not reflect additional charges that can change based on your credit, mortgage insurance, and property taxes.

I have to caution people about getting in over your head by putting too little down. Just because you think you can afford it today, that doesn't mean that you will be able to afford it tomorrow. Talk with your lender about all the options available. Just remember, *don't get in over your head*.

REPRESENTATION

This is your real-estate agent we are talking about. Your agent had better be good! This person needs to know absolutely everything about you in regard to what you like structurally and what supports your lifestyle… *everything!* This person should have your best interest at heart and is legally bound to that interest. So many agents out there are just trying to make money, but once you've found the right one for you, make sure you stick with him or her. Your agent needs to be competent and have all the knowledge about the area memorized. Remember, these people are supposed to be the experts; there is no room for mediocracy when potentially purchasing something you'll likely be living in for thirty years. Find someone who fits you and your life.

NEGOTIATION SKILLS AND STYLE

Find an agent who fits your personality. For example, if the guy or gal is a hotshot type and is most interested in closing a deal as fast as possible, that can't possibly be in your best interest. This agent might be the best and the hottest in the company, but he or she is not the right fit for you if you want (and you should!) to go slow and be careful to make sure you don't drop into any pitfalls. In other words, a house can be a money trap. You might have termites. You might have rodents. You might have wood rot or lead pipes or mold. You might have drainage or flooding problems. All this is in addition to the basic integrity of the house itself: roof, appliances, heating and cooling system, and so on. There can be a whole slew of terrible problems, all very costly. So, especially if this is your first house, you *need* to go slow.

PRICE

Remember, just because you were approved for "X" amount, that doesn't mean that you should spend "X" amount. There is a common term called "house poor" that refers to people living in homes (for whatever reason) above their comfortable financial level. This means that something needs to be sacrificed in order to live in this better home, something that is no doubt valuable to health, well-being, and tranquility. You want to avoid buying a home (let alone anything) where you are stretched so thin that you do not have enough money to do anything else in life other than work to pay your mortgage. Don't buy something so expensive that you are not able to enjoy other aspects of your life and can't afford to travel, eat out, or partake in other activities that you enjoy solely because you are anchored to your mortgage.

> "Ten million dollars after I became a star I was deeply in debt."
>
> —SAMMY DAVIS JR.

PLAN FOR UNEXPECTED EXPENSES

Everybody's heard of Murphy's Law. What this means is that if something *can* go wrong, it generally *does*. And when it does, it is not covered by insurance. Now what? This is why having savings is important. It is more important to have savings for an emergency than to feel that you are a person of status. The savings should serve a real and essential purpose, namely to get you out of some unforeseen and important dilemma, which can range from unexpected air-conditioner or heater repairs to unexpected pipe bursts, to any other number of things.

When looking to buy a home, you should have all the knowledge available to you. So I have included a pros and cons section to compare renting with buying. Let's face it; maybe it's not the right time for you to buy a home, and renting may be the best option. At least you have something to contemplate while waiting to buy.

RENTING PROS

Easy, no commitment, landlord pays expenses. The reason most people rent is that it's way cheaper than buying, and you can look at a condo and potentially move into it on the same day. Renting pros are all related to mere convenience. The commitment is usually six to twelve months, and you can then find a new place or continue renting. If any expenses come up or things break, you can make a phone call, and someone will come out to fix them. It is much easier to be a renter!

RENTING CONS

Money *wasted*. The major savings of home ownership come from the fact that real estate generally appreciates. Even in a down market, which is fairly rare, you can wait till there's an upturn in the market. But the bottom line is that you have an asset (unlike your car) that increases in value each year. So those who rent are paying almost the same amount as the average mortgage and are getting nothing for it but a month of shelter and a handful of rent-payment receipts. Owning a house, you can make hundreds of thousands of dollars you would not otherwise have if you remained a lifelong tenant.

I want you to think about this in terms of what you get in return when you rent. Say you live in a condo that costs $1,000 a month, and you sign up for a twelve-month lease. At the end of one year, you've paid out $12,000 into your landlord's bank account. What did you get out of it? You got to sleep there, eat there, shower there, and have a place to store your stuff! When you move out, you get nothing from the property. Just remember that the $12,000 you spent is gone, bye-bye; you'll never see that again! Think about this.

OWNING PROS

Pride of ownership. If you own your own property, you have the pride of owning a property of your own. You work in a way that is much more gratifying. There are numerous advantages to buying a home or condo. Appreciation of your property value (remember that the world is not producing any more land!) is another advantage. People are cranking kids out at an exponential rate, and they will all need a place to sleep!

Once the property is paid off, you have endless possibilities concerning what you can do with it. Remember that people will *always* need a place to live. You could potentially rent out the property and create a new source of income for yourself.

OWNING CONS

You must pay all the expenses if you're renting out space; you need to be concerned about vacancies and liabilities.

People who own real estate will tell you that it's not easy, but it's worth it! When you're just starting out and things break, finances start to get real tight.

Ownership also comes with paying property taxes to that state. Be sure to look into this when looking to purchase.

THREE WAYS TO MAKE MONEY OFF OWNING A HOME

1. PRINCIPAL/MORTGAGE PAYMENTS
In a stable market, and with a $200,000 loan, you no doubt will be paying off about $6,000 to $8,000 *per year* in principal (the noninterest portion of the actual loan repayment). This is money you can regain when you sell the house, or that you will be able to borrow against in the future. Look at how much will accrue in ten or twenty years! This is a huge advantage over the situation of renters, where they wind up with only a handful of rent receipts.

At the end of each year, your loan will have decreased by "X," and you will add that much to your net worth. Think of your home as your own bank; you're paying the principal down, which in turn can be viewed as a bank account.

2. TAX DEDUCTION
The interest that you are paying on the loan can be deducted from your income taxes at the end of the year. The interest on the loan is one of many ways to deduct taxes from your income depending whether the

property is bought as a primary residence or as an investment property. Depending on what state you live in, you will need to pay property taxes. Property taxes can be deducted from your income tax, which saves you even more money. I am no tax expert, but these are things that you should be aware of as an extra way of making income on real estate. You can write off the interest on your taxes, therefore lowering your taxes. The point here is that you can deduct the interest and taxes you spend on your home (property) from your personal income tax. Renters have no such privilege.

3. APPRECIATION AND RENOVATIONS
Now, let's say you buy a house for $200,000. History has its ups and downs in regard to appreciation. Depending on the market, you can find your property increase in value anywhere from 5 to 15 percent per year. This too is a huge advantage and another great reason to buy instead of rent.

REASONS YOU DON'T OWN NOW
I've talked to so many people about the idea of buying real estate, and all their fears and concerns about the investment are valid. I agree; buying a home and having that commitment to one location is daunting. So let's go through some of the main concerns so you realize that you're not the only one with this predicament.

1. IT'S NOT A DECISION TO BE TAKEN LIGHTLY
Many people are hesitant about making the tough decision to purchase something so costly. And since it is usually only done up to maybe three times in a lifetime, it is a significant decision. The homework involved and the self-analysis of where you want to live are major things to consider.

2. IT'S A LARGE COMMITMENT
You are obligated to pay your mortgage monthly, and if for some reason you fail to do so, you can lose the house. Usually, if you are forced to sell

due to nonpayment of your mortgage, you won't make as much money as if you were up to date on your payments. There are many factors that bear on this kind of a desperate sale.

3. You've Never Done It—Just a Little Scared
Odd as it may seem, this psychological factor is very prevalent. Many people are just not very comfortable doing something that they have never done before. Yet all the positive factors we've listed for buying the house are still in play. You need to overcome the unfamiliar. This is normal for such a huge purchase. Nonetheless, the facts bear out that you are *foolish to rent if you can buy!* This is foreign territory, and since you've never done this, of course it's frightening.

4. You Don't Know How
This again comes under the category of fear and hesitation, because you have never done it before. You're simply unfamiliar with the process and the potential pitfalls. Still, understanding the positive benefits should be enough to overcome these psychological obstacles.

Buying a home, for most people, is not something you do every day. Therefore, most of us are unfamiliar with the latest trends, rules, laws, and so on. This is why you should be able to rely mostly on a good real-estate agent. Remember that the most important trait of a good agent is that he or she is an honest person and incredibly knowledgeable.

EXTRA REASONS TO BUY

Pride of Ownership
This is something that appeals to the very basic instinct of pride. You are proud to show and invite people to your new home. It makes you feel successful, and it gives you roots you may not have had before. So you can see that the money you have invested in your home is like putting the

money into your own piggy bank—rather than throwing that money out the window towards rent!

RENOVATION

Let's suppose that you need, or want, a new kitchen or bathroom or floors or paint. People like new homes, but if you purchase an older home that needs work, then you can "build" it the way you want. A home's structure might not be brand-new, but the paint, floors, kitchen, and bathrooms can be remodeled and redone to make it "new" for you. If you don't have the money up front to immediately remodel, who cares? Wait and save money to do the remodel down the road; there is no rush! Just remind yourself that the money is now going back into your pocket, and one day the home will be paid off. Over time, you can do projects here and there to bring the value of the property up. Ultimately, these renovations will both make it more fun to live there and increase the home's value.

CHAPTER 7

• • •

INVESTMENTS

I'VE MENTIONED THIS many times already. The world revolves around money! The entire purpose of this book is to communicate that *your* world should not revolve around money and, at the same time, show that money will provide you a more comfortable life when you are retiring. Many people wandering through life right now may not have a choice of whether they can retire or not. You don't want to have to work later in life when you should be relaxing and reaping the benefits of your working years. It's extremely important to think past this Friday or the next month, and think about ten, twenty, or thirty years from now. It may not be easy, but it is *very* important.

When I talk to people about investments and building wealth, they always refer to the stock market as the number-one form of investment. People have this idea that the stock market is the only kind of investment opportunity that is available. I will explain later that you have alternative options, but you must open your eyes and do some research to set your retirement up properly. I tell you, nobody will take care of you better than you will take care of yourself. If you think the government is in place to make sure you have a warm bed to sleep in and food in your stomach, then you will have a rude awakening.

Let's talk about investing and where you should start. I always ask this question: do you go to a plumber to buy a diamond ring for your wife? The answer is always no! My point here is that no one should invest money in something they know absolutely nothing about. So the next topic is stockbrokers, or professionals in the field. It's great to seek out people who are much smarter in an area you are thinking about entering.

Remember, the stockbroker makes money (a lot, in fact) off people like you and me. The reality is that most of the time, they get paid when you buy and sell stock! Some stock options give the broker a higher commission—sometimes two "points" in and two "points" out (two points meaning 2 percent of the total investment you make with them). Do you think a stockbroker wants to sell you stocks that he or she gets a smaller commission on? They don't have your best interest in mind or whether or not you go bankrupt in the process of attempting to gain wealth. My last point is, if you're going to invest, make sure you do your homework. Below are just a few things you can educate yourself on to help you build your wealth.

THE VALUE OF THE DOLLAR

Even if you can only save fifty or one hundred dollars a month, is it really worth it? I'm going to show you that the answer is yes! People have a hard time setting aside five dollars here or five dollars there, but the fact of the matter is, *it all adds up*. We the people have lost the concept of, and respect for, the dollar. We do not understand the value of the dollar and how the wealth-accumulation process starts. Someone younger than me saw me stop in the middle of a parking lot to pick up a penny and saw how I was so excited to do so. He said, "Did you know it's not even worth your time to pick up a penny?" I said, "Tell me you're kidding!" This idiot began to tell me how my energy was not worth the time to bend down and pick up the penny. I told him, "See, you're the problem. You don't understand the value of a dollar (or in this case a penny)!" People know that the dollar is made up of one hundred pennies, but they don't actually see the link between the penny and the dollar. Therefore, they don't value the penny mentally. Most of the population buys things via electronic purchases (or through credit or debit cards), so they don't actually see a "dollar" being exchanged for goods. This is due to our online banking world and electronic exchanges. What they see is a piece of plastic being swiped and no actual dollars being exchanged. Hence, we have a spending-and-debt issue in today's society.

What I want you to understand is the power of compound interest and how to create a "buy in" for you to begin thinking about the future and achieving serenity and financial stability. There is a popular ad on TV that shows, quite graphically, that if a young person begins saving twenty dollars a month toward retirement, he or she will eventually amass a veritable fortune because of compound interest. The problem is, of course, who in their youth thinks about retirement? This "out of sight, out of mind" mentality is the problem. But I'll cover more of this topic later… now back to how all your pennies add up.

So you have your money and are ready to invest. You've determined how much you will put aside and when you will need your money. You've taken care of your debt and determined your goals. Now it's time for you to find out what investments are right for you to meet your goals.

COMPOUND INTEREST

By starting to save now, you're giving your money—however little it is—time to earn compound interest, which means that you can contribute less money for fewer years if you start when you're young and still end up with more cash than someone who waits to save later in their life. Remember earlier in the book (from the credit-card chapter) how the interest accumulated more and more every month? This is the same concept, but it is now working in your favor.

Let me give you an example. If you start saving or investing when you're twenty-five, save $100 a month for ten years, and then let the money sit, your stash will grow to $174,928 by the time you turn sixty-five (assuming an 8 percent annual return). If you wait until age thirty-five to start saving and save the same $100 a month for the next thirty years, you'll have only $135,940 by age sixty-five (at the same rate). You will have contributed three times as much starting later but will end up with nearly $39,000 less. So you see here, just because you're saving doesn't actually mean you're getting the max efficiency out of your "penny." You need to learn to make your money work for you. The table below provides a graphic example of precisely how this works. In this case, it demonstrates how compound interest (at a 5 percent rate) adds up over the course of just one year.

Year	Starting Value	Interest Rate	Monthly Interest Earned	End Value
1	$100.00	5%	$5.00	$105.00
2	$105.00	5%	$5.25	$110.25
3	$110.25	5%	$5.51	$115.76
4	$115.76	5%	$5.79	$121.55
5	$121.55	5%	$6.08	$127.63
6	$127.63	5%	$6.38	$134.01
7	$134.01	5%	$6.70	$140.71
8	$140.71	5%	$7.04	$147.75
9	$147.75	5%	$7.39	$155.13
10	$155.13	5%	$7.76	$162.89
11	$162.89	5%	$8.14	$171.03
12	$171.03	5%	$8.55	$179.59

SAVINGS ACCOUNTS

If you save your money in a savings account, the bank or credit union will pay you interest, and you can easily get your money whenever you want it. At most banks, your savings account will be insured by the Federal Deposit Insurance Corporation (FDIC) up to $250,000. In the past, you could get about 2.5 percent a year ($2.50 for every $100) for all the money you had in your account. The markets change, and so do the interest rates that banks pay you. The point to make here is that savings accounts pay interest on the money you have stored with them. This is because they take your money and loan it out to other people who need money. The bank will use your money and charge a greater interest rate to be able to make a profit for the bank; then they will pay you interest on your money that they used to lend out to other people.

INSURED BANK MONEY-MARKET ACCOUNTS

These accounts tend to offer higher interest rates than savings accounts and often give you free check-writing privileges. Like a savings account, many money-market accounts will be insured by the FDIC. Note that bank money-market accounts are not the same as money-market mutual funds, which are not insured by the FDIC.

CERTIFICATES OF DEPOSIT (CDS)

You can earn an even higher interest rate if you put your money in a certificate of deposit, or CD, which is also protected by the FDIC. When you buy a CD, you promise that you're going to keep your money in the bank for a certain amount of time and earn 1 to 4 percent off compounded interest. CDs fluctuate all the time, but for the most part you will get a higher rate of return on a CD than on a savings account. CDs are a guaranteed safe investment.

BONDS

Many companies borrow money so that they can become even bigger and more successful. One way they borrow money is by selling bonds. When you, the consumer, buy a bond, you're lending your money to the company so that it can grow. The company promises to pay you interest and to return your money on a future date. The company's "promise" to repay your principal thus generally makes bonds less risky than stocks. But bonds can be risky as well. To assess how risky a bond is, you can check the bond's credit rating. Unlike stockholders, bondholders know how much money they will make, unless the company goes out of business. If the company goes out of business or declares bankruptcy, bondholders may lose their money. But if there is any money left in the company, they will get their investment back before the stockholders. Bonds generally provide higher returns (but with higher risk) than savings accounts, but they also have lower returns (along with lower risk) than stocks.

TREASURY NOTES

Treasury notes are securities that have a stated interest rate that is paid semiannually until maturity. What makes notes and bonds different is the length of the terms until maturity. Notes are issued in two-, three-, five-, and ten-year terms. Conversely, bonds are long-term investments with terms of greater than ten years.

Treasury bills, or T-bills, are sold in terms ranging from a few days to fifty-two weeks. Bills are typically sold at a discount from the paramount (also called face value). For instance, you might pay $990 for a $1,000 bill. When the bill matured, you would be paid $1,000. The difference between the purchase price and the face value is interest. They are one of the few money-market instruments that are affordable to individual investors. T-bills are usually issued in denominations of $1,000, $5,000, $10,000, $25,000, $50,000, $100,000, and $1 million, up to a maximum purchase of $5 million, and commonly have maturities of one month (four weeks), three months (thirteen weeks), or six months (twenty-six weeks).

The interest is the difference between the purchase price and either the price paid at maturity (face value) or the price of the bill if sold prior to maturity. For example, let's say you buy a thirteen-week T-bill priced at $9,800. Essentially, the US government (and its nearly bulletproof credit rating) writes you an IOU for $10,000 that it agrees to pay back in three months. The appreciation—and, therefore, the value to you—comes from the difference between the discounted value you originally paid and the amount you receive back ($10,000). In this case, the T-bill pays a 2.04 percent interest rate ($200/$9,800 = 2.04 percent) over a three-month period. Now, it's critical to remember that these rates change over time! What I am writing about now may change just a year from now. What I want you to understand is the concept of how these investments are marketed to you and how you get paid based on the amount you invest.

The biggest reason that T-bills are so popular is that they (and all Treasuries) are considered the safest investments in the world, because the US government backs them. In fact, they are considered risk-free and are exempt from state and local taxes.

STOCKS

Before we talk about how to invest in the stock market, consider your prejudices. What springs to mind immediately is a really smart person who knows—yes, he *really* knows—the market. He knows what to buy and what to sell, but most importantly he knows *when* to buy and *when* to sell. Then there's some age-old wisdom that says, "The stock market is for people who have too much money and don't know what to do with it." This kind of thinking sort of dismantles the image of a guy starting with a hundred dollars and winding up a billionaire.

Just remember this. No matter how much you or your broker (who gets a hefty commission for the privilege of selling you stock) know about the companies you are investing in, you can't possibly know the inside workings of the companies or how they are run. Sure, you can check all the stats about earnings and dividends, but there are so many variables that you can't possibly foresee. Things like business climate, world markets, and so on ensure that there is always some element of gambling involved—*certainly* not like Las Vegas or anything, just not a 100 percent guarantee.

When you buy stock in a company, you become one of the owners. Your share of the company depends on how many shares of the company's stock you own. Over the past sixty years, the investment that has provided the highest average rate of return has been stocks. But as mentioned, there are no guarantees of profits when you buy stock, which makes stock one of the riskiest investments available to you. If the company doesn't do well or falls out of favor with investors, your stock can fall in price, and you can lose all your money.

You can make money in two ways from stock. First, the price of the stock can rise if the company does well and other investors want to buy the company's stock. If a stock rises from ten dollars to twelve dollars, the two-dollar increase is called a capital gain or appreciation. Secondly, a company sometimes pays out a part of its profits (a dividend) to stockholders in the company. Sometimes a company will decide not to pay out dividends, choosing instead to keep its profits and use them to expand the business, build new factories, design better products, or hire more workers. It's important to remember here that you can make money on the stock price going up, but you can also lose money on the stock price going down!

> Unless you can watch your investment in stocks go down
> by 50 percent you should not be in the stock market.

—WARREN BUFFETT

Stocks that pay out a dividend have several advantages over those that do not. Dividend-paying stocks provide a more certain income than what price appreciation alone offers. When the stock market declines, holders of dividend-paying stocks still receive an income, and the dividend helps maintain the stock price even in a down market.

And, often, the dividend plus the capital gains of a dividend-paying stock is greater than the capital gains of many stocks that do not pay a dividend. In fact, dividends have accounted for about 40 percent of the total return of the stock market since 1928!

The downside is that the dividend earnings are not only taxed immediately, but they're also taxed twice. For example, suppose a company has a strong sales year and announces that it will pay a dividend of one dollar per share to its shareholders. Before it does that, however, it must pay corporate taxes on its earnings. Assuming a total 30 percent tax bracket, the one-dollar dividend has just been reduced to only seventy cents actually received by the shareholders per share. The seventy-cent share rate will also be taxed on the individual shareholders' tax returns (these are your returns). If an investor is in a combined (federal and state) tax bracket of forty percent, then there goes an additional twenty-eight cents lost to taxes. So, of the one-dollar announced dividend, the investor is left with less than half that amount after taxes—only forty-two cents, to be exact. But perhaps, "a bird in the hand is worth two in the bush." And it is an indication that companies are truly financially successful when they actually have money to pay the dividends (it's not just profits on paper).

Many large corporations provide dividend reinvestment plans (DRIPs) for their stock. These programs allow investors to buy company shares directly from the company, void of all brokerage commissions, and the company will reinvest the dividends into additional company stock. In fact, dividends can be used to buy fractional shares of stock.

> Investing should be like watching paint dry or grass
> grow. If you want excitement go to Las Vegas.
>
> —PAUL SAMUELSON

Most companies also allow partial participation where the stockholder can specify the amount to be reinvested and the amount to be paid as cash. While DRIPs are excellent investment vehicles, they differ from stock dividends in that taxes are due on the reinvested dividends in the year that the dividends are earned. And, of course, you pay tax again if you ultimately sell the stock.

RETIREMENT ACCOUNTS

Roth IRA accounts are an option that allows you to be taxed this year on money you set aside for retirement, and when you take it out at retirement age, you are not taxed. The benefit? You get taxed up front and then have unlimited potential on that money to gain interest and never get taxed on the profits. This is one of the best ways the government has set up retirement for the public. The reason why the government only allows $5,500 per person per year is that they understand the "opportunity cost" of this money being compounded over someone's lifetime. Of course, you need to *invest* the money to truly see the benefit.

A "traditional" IRA is the same as a Roth IRA, except that you are deducting the money from your annual income each year and will be taxed on the money when you pull it out at retirement age. Now that may sound good for the short term, but keep in mind that taxes will most likely not go down in the future. Obviously, they are far more likely to go up. This makes the option to be taxed now in the Roth IRA option very appealing. The hope is that you do not withdraw funds until after retirement, when, hopefully, you are in a smaller tax bracket.

WASTEFUL SPENDING

If you're thinking you don't have enough money to invest, think again. What if you could cut out some wasteful spending every month? That extra money could provide the basis for investing, or at least something to get you started. There are many ways of avoiding wasteful spending:

- Trim subscriptions
- Pay your bills on time
- Learn to cook (*big-time savings*)
- Change your calling plan
- Use free media online
- Cancel your gym membership if you don't use it
- Raise your car-insurance deductible (might save you some money per month)
- Pay off your credit card
- Bundle programs for multiple services
- Avoid overpriced coffee establishments

Keep track of your money. The best way to save is to know what you spend. It might not be pretty, but detail every expense for a month to get an idea of where you can cut back. Nearly everyone has some fat they can trim from their spending to put toward a savings goal. I'm not worried about the money you have accounted for and know where it's going; I'm worried about the money you spent without knowing where it went.

The greatest piece of advice I can give you is this: "It's not how much money you make, but how much money you spend, that determines your wealth." My stepmother Terry used to tell me this at a young age.

And, as my grandfather always told me, "Success listens to success."

KEYS TO SUCCESS

CHAPTER 8

• • •

SUCCESS IN LIFE-QUALITIES, TRAITS, HABITS, AND GOALS

WHAT IF I told you that today is the day to make a difference in your life, to take full responsibility for the past and start creating your future? This is the day you decide the excuses aren't working anymore. That moment when you're done listening to yourself complain about your job, your living situation, and your relationships.

When we take responsibility for our *life*, doors start opening that we never imagined could. It's true. And it's time. No matter where you live, where you were raised, or how much money you make. Your gender, ethnicity, and weight have nothing to do with the choice of making a change for the better. Owning where you're at right *now* is all the confidence it takes to pave a new path.

I am going to teach you how to take responsibility for your life. I am going to show you just how capable you really are—just how very *free*, in fact, you are.

The truth is that it's easy to hang our heads and tell sad stories about all the ways that life has set us up for defeat and limits us. We've even got plenty of past experiences to "prove" it! But there comes a time in every person's life when a decision needs to be made, an imperative question addressed head-on. And the question is this: Am I going to let my past define my future? Am I willing to remain captive to past failures? Or do I want something *better*—something *more*?

Insanity: Doing the same thing over and over again and
expecting different results.

—Albert Einstein

I mean, c'mon. Take it from this genius. Stop the cycle! Learn the lesson. Your thoughts and actions create your future. Embrace the change! I'm here to show you the way out, to provide tools and strategies for designing your path. And most of all, I'm here to remind you that you really *can* achieve more than you can imagine.

YOU ARE IN CONTROL

"I want to take action, but I don't know what action to take or which direction to take it in. I'm no Einstein. I'm no Warren Buffett, either. My resources are limited; I'm afraid to take that risk or take that job…"

You see what just happened? You just spiraled back to square one. *Stop that!* We put a man on the moon when people said it couldn't be done, and we can now talk face-to-face with someone on the other side of the planet. Don't tell me that your position is so bad that you can't get out! What you need is a good sense of who you are and where you're headed. A road map to get there. This is the *best way* to regain control of your life, and it's surprisingly simple.

So now you know that success is a choice. Let's get to work on a plan to establish *new habits*, habits that will help you to your own success. Now, commit yourself to make the changes. It's time to think differently, act differently, and take full responsibility for yourself.

Decide what you want. This sounds much simpler than it is. But this is the first step to success. You know very well where you are now; but without a clear view of where you want to be, how on earth can you begin moving toward it? Be specific here. Assess where you are now and where you want to be in the future. Use the back of this book. There are blank pages for you to start taking notes.

If you want to be a business owner, decide what sort of business you wish to run. What product or service does it offer? Whom does it cater to? In other words, don't just say, "I want to own a business." Say, "I want to open an artisan bagel shop in Manhattan." Or, "I want to own a scuba company down in the Bahamas and help big Hollywood films, like Stuart Cove." See the difference? So ask yourself: What do I really *want*?

Be clear about what is happening *now*. And where you *want* to eventually be.

Set specific goals. Now that you know what you want, sit down and really think about how to get to there from here. Break the big ideas down into bite-sized chunks. Don't stop until the actions you have listed are manageable and unintimidating. Then, put them on a timeline. Set daily goals, monthly goals, and annual goals. Use quantifiable numbers with real dates and expectations. This gives you a full view of your new plan, allowing you to gauge progress and celebrate achievement. Let's look at a few examples of how this might work in its application.

Daily task list: Run two miles. Check e-mail from 8:00 to 9:00 a.m. Drop job application at [list specific locations]. Networking event at 7:00 p.m.

Weekly plans: Schedule appointment for an oil change. Get the oil changed on primary vehicle. Call to check in on the family. Weekend hike.

Yearly goals: Pay off the car entirely. Save $500–$1,000 and store it somewhere I can get at it in case of an emergency. Save $5,000 in general savings. Land a new job in [specific industry].

As you can see, making these lists is not only easy, it can also be a *lot* of fun, and it gives you a sense of accomplishment when you check things off! The trick, though, is to *actually make the lists!* Don't just read about them here, nod in understanding, and then move on to the next chapter. Do whatever it takes to *take the time* to put these steps into effect. Starting right now—today—make your lists. Make your lists, and then get into the habit of expanding on them *daily*. This is not just a "clever tip"—it will change your life!

Write Everything Down: This is super important. Whether we're talking about developing new ideas, building strategies, or making to-do lists, write everything down, or you are bound to forget it! Buy a whiteboard, keep a journal, invest in a planner, or download a project-management application to your smartphone. Whatever you decide to use, make sure that all of this is going down on paper, so to speak. This will help you stay focused, inspired, and effective. And one more thing on this subject: whatever you decide to use, be sure that it is *in your face*—unavoidable. Writing things down is all about evading forgetfulness. But if your to-do lists, business ideas, and appointments are just getting stuffed in some corner of your messy desk—if they aren't constantly getting in your way— then *you will forget about them* even though they're written down. "Out of sight, out of mind," as the old saying goes. And it's absolutely true.

So if you're using a whiteboard, mount it right above your bed or office desk. If you're using a planner, take it everywhere you go. If you're using an application on your phone, let it be a prominent member of your home screen. If you have a to-do list, find a way to keep that list before you at all times throughout the day until your tasks have been completed. This is one area where you are encouraged to get in your own way. It will make all the difference.

Get Healthy and Stay That Way: Healthier means happier. Your body is a "machine," and it must be maintained! Get plenty of sleep and adjust your diet to support a happier, healthier lifestyle. Finally, you can't neglect exercise. Remember: changing the course of your life begins with changing you. This may not be easy at first, but it will be productive if you stick with it. Being healthy does not happen by accident. It requires ambition and hard work.

There's another important point to be made here. Developing healthy habits and supporting a healthy lifestyle are not the same as making drastic changes in diet or exercise. This is not the time to jump on board the latest diet fad or workout regimen. What we're looking for here is sustainable change. Start slow and build yourself up to this—otherwise you'll just burn yourself out. Remember, this is about establishing new habits that will bring about true, lasting change.

So do your research and find something that works for you. The important thing here is to *actually do the work*. Take the steps that are necessary for you to become healthy and vital, and then keep on taking them. This is a lifestyle change. Quitting is not an option.

Read, Read, Read: Let's face it; most people do not enjoy reading. Perhaps this is because they feel that it isn't interesting enough or that it's a waste of time. The reason for this is simple: *they're not reading about what's interesting to them*. Whether or not you naturally enjoy reading— *do this!* Read articles and tutorials online related to your interests and chosen path. Read biographies and success stories. Open your mind to receive new information. Seek it out, in fact. Allow yourself to become hungry for new ideas from all-new sources. Devour this new content! Be inspired by it! *Find what you love and immerse yourself in it*. Let it take root in your mind and watch as it helps you think more creatively and act more efficiently.

Get Smart with Networking: Surround yourself with people who are smarter than you. This is one of the most important "success secrets" you will ever hear. Here's another one: if you're the smartest person in the room, you're in the wrong room. My point is that you should surround yourself with people who are serious about success and self-improvement. If they are smarter than you, better than you, more successful than you, this will absolutely speed up your own progress. It will push you to become more. Let go of your ego and open your circle to like-minded individuals who lead by example. You just might learn something!

Your Word: Generations before us, entire empires were built on a handshake. A man's word was his bond. People took their work seriously.

They understood that personal and professional shortcomings such as laziness, tardiness, and shoddy workmanship weakened their reputation. These days, we've learned to spend nearly as much time on CYA (Cover Your Ass) as on the actual work we've agreed to. We're all too familiar with the "fine print" of lengthy contracts, and we've all been bitten by those "snakes in the grass."

Become a person of your word, and you instantly set yourself apart from most of your competition. Give the people in your life—both personally and professionally—the gift of being able to depend on you, and you will begin to build a foundation that cannot be shaken; you begin to build a solid reputation. "A man is only as good as his word." This is why commitment is so important, especially in today's world.

Converting these tips into real action will require a ton of willpower. These actions will feel unnatural and forced at first—establishing new habits always does—but if you continue following this course and *do not quit*, then each of these new challenges will become second nature. And they will be the tools that, piece by piece, construct a better, happier, more productive, and more fulfilled version of you.

CAUTION: DON'T BE A FAKER

This is very important: don't just read about, think about, or talk about these things (your goals, these lessons, new habits, etc.)—do them! Take real action. Too many people are chronic *conceptual* risk-takers; they make a habit of considering effective action (some even come up with brilliant ideas), but they never take any real action. These people are all talk, but they never find the guts to actually change their behavior. These people are conceptual risk-takers but actual cowards. Do not trick yourself into becoming one of these.

You must always say what you mean and mean what you say. You need to be absolutely honest—not just with others, but also with yourself. Commit to change and then stick with that commitment. Be unafraid to look yourself in the eye. Assume *responsibility* for yourself. Never forget; this is your life; it is not okay to just quit. You must decide on a course and then pursue that course with all the strength and passion that you can muster.

Acting in this way—taking responsibility for yourself and your commitments—is what helps develop true inner power and your self-esteem. The harder you work toward establishing beneficial habits and changing the course of your life, the more you will come to respect the person you see in the mirror. You will begin to draw strength and confidence from your actions. You will begin to trust yourself, and this foundation of trust will allow you to become even more effective, even more confident, even more capable.

Self-improvement is not a linear path; it is compounding. The more you allow yourself to grow, the faster you will grow. The harder you work, the harder you are able to work, the more you are capable of achieving. And it all starts with laying a purposeful foundation of unwavering intention and effective habits. Adjust your thinking, change your habits, and you will improve your life. You may not have ever heard this before today, but you cannot unhear it now: *you* are in control. You have everything you need to take a stand and change. Literally. Everything.

A QUICK WORD ON FAILURE

As you move into this new way of thinking and acting, it is inevitable that you will—at some point—fail. It is incredibly important for you to know that failing does not make you a failure. These are two very different things. Failing is a natural consequence of learning something new. It's called trial and error. In fact, it's half the battle, isn't it? But failing does not define who you are.

When you fail (and you will), the key is to pick yourself back up and try again. Do this over and over and over, and you will find that, before long, you have succeeded. So failure may be natural and necessary; but it is not who you are. You are the daring pioneer standing up to failure and ensuring its defeat.

SUCCESS = Timing + Talent + Tenacity + Dedication.

—POPS

CHAPTER 9

• • •

COMMUNICATION

Your ability to convey your ideas to others will be an
enormous determinant to your success"

—Warren Buffett

We are turning into hermits and quickly losing our social skills. I've been walking down the street and passed a total stranger, and I've said hello. Their nonverbal response says to me, *Do I know you?* but they standoffishly mutter, "Hello." My point is, do I need to know you just to say hello? This is also a good one: when I get into an elevator now, rarely do I get someone who says hello before me! Depending on my mood, I will bring up the fact that we as a country have gotten so disconnected from being social human beings that a casual hello is quickly fading! This must stop. We can all agree that because of our access to social media and instant communications on our cell phones, we are slowly fading from being social in public. Maybe this chapter can help you become a better communicator and open your eyes a little.

Effective communication is the key to get you to where you want to be in your life. Maybe you've heard that before and brushed it off as just a cliché. Huge mistake! In fact, without the ability to effectively communicate, your chances of finding any kind of success in life—either with money or on a personal level—are basically zero. I'm not suggesting that you need to be a whiz at public speaking or an extroverted personality type. My point, rather, is that *words matter.* People make all kinds of inferences about you, both fairly and unfairly, not to mention consciously and subliminally, based on the words you use and the way you present yourself to the world with both your body language and the way that you speak.

Unfortunately, despite all our futuristic electronics and "interconnectivity," in reality, people are more disconnected from one another than ever before. The art of casual conversation, of actually speaking face-to-face with friends and neighbors, is being steadily chipped away. Texting and e-mail have their place, but they should never replace human contact. Think of the last time you spoke with a stranger, maybe something as simple as riding together on the same elevator. Did anyone say hello to you? Or do they (or do you) reserve that only for acquaintances? To me, that's a major problem that is almost completely overlooked in this era of social media. The ability to strike up a conversation, even small talk, with strangers as well as people we know is quickly dwindling. It's as though people are hiding behind computer keyboards and smartphones to avoid human contact, whether they recognize it or not. Don't fall into that trap. A nation of hermits will never be a nation of winners. Be deliberate about the whole concept of communications. It's more than just a trait to claim on your résumé; it's one of those real-life skills that they never teach you at school but will pay gigantic dividends to you throughout your life.

Have no doubt about it; communication is essential for building successful business and personal relationships. It has an impact whenever it occurs—we can use communication to influence every interaction in a positive way, but only by developing the skills needed to communicate effectively. You can also use communication ineffectively. Take for instance, the phrase, "Excuse me." Depending on your tone of voice, this can come off very respectfully, or, if said with certain emphasis, it could indicate that you are offended, and you could come off unfriendly.

The ability to connect and build rapport with other people is a foundational life skill, and you should ideally be actively developing it from an early age. It is a learned skill and can be learned (and used) at any age. An example of this can be found in the use of the word *only*. Consider the different intonations you can put on that word. For example, you could say, "If only I knew that." This suggests you might have reacted differently. Or you could say, "If only I knew that," with the emphasis on the I, suggesting that things would be different if you were the only person who "knew that."

Communication is an exchange of information between individuals or groups of people. It's a process in which we try, as clearly and accurately as we can, to convey our thoughts, intentions, and objectives. It is successful only when both the sender and the receiver understand the same information. Although it's become increasingly important to have good communication skills in this highly informational and technological environment, many individuals continue to struggle with this idea. When they are unable to communicate effectively, they are held back both in their careers and in their personal relationships.

When we use the word *communication*, we are referring to verbal and nonverbal communication. Verbal and nonverbal language are essential elements for committed relationships, friendships, business relationships, and virtually all other kinds of relationships. We depend on making ourselves understood to convey our wants and needs, likes and dislikes, and thoughts and feelings, and to make requests of others.

We communicate nonverbally with our faces and our bodies. For example, when we are listening, we might tilt our heads a bit or lean toward the speaker. The speaker, seeing this, would likely perceive us to be interested and listening attentively to him or her. Conversely, if we fidget, sigh, roll our eyes, or make any of a number of faces with our mouths and lips (you know what I mean!), the speaker could accurately perceive us to be in disagreement, contemptuous, critical, disapproving, or just plain disinterested. Use hand gestures carefully; you should be conscious of what your hands are saying as you speak. Some hand gestures can be very effective in highlighting your points, and others can be distracting (or even offensive!) to some listeners. For example, finger pointing. This can mean that the person is using the finger either for emphasis on a specific object or as an accusatory gesture.

We communicate verbally with the words we choose, along with the inflection, pitch, decibel level, and cadence with which we speak them. And make no mistake about it; a speaker's attitude comes across loud and clear when he or she speaks.

Be true to your beliefs, but do not judge, become overly emotional, or refuse to listen fully because you are so eager to convince the other person. In other words, you do not want to be more interested in what you have to *say* than in what you are being *told*. It has to do with the art of conversation and the equal amount of give-and-take in good social communication. You will have many conversations with people who do not share the same beliefs as you, and that's okay. Just remember the golden rule: *don't be an asshole!*

COMMUNICATION TOPICS TO REMEMBER:

- Personal space. It is hard to talk when you are ten feet apart, but you do not want to be six inches apart either. Generally speaking, two to three feet is a comfortable distance for most people in the United States. Other cultures around the world have differing opinions on what is too close. In other cultures, it is acceptable to be very close. This space changes with how and where you were brought up.
- Express your concerns nonjudgmentally. Talk about your questions or concerns without blaming other people. Explain constructively what you expect and why you expect it.
- *I* versus *You*. If you've ever been in an argument with someone who is difficult to speak with, and you start a statement with *you*, the person immediately gets defensive. Rather than saying, "You didn't explain that very well," say, "I didn't understand what you just said. Please explain it again." Starting with *you* makes it even harder to progress to the rest of the conversation. Choose the

words you use at the beginning of the sentence wisely if you are trying to make a point.

- Listen with a purpose. In a work environment, if you just pay "lip service," people will become increasingly skeptical of what you have to say and may not even listen to you at all. Be attentive. Concentrate on what is being said.

- Reflect back. Restating what has been said helps the speaker know that you understand and that you're interested!

- Share the conversation. Don't be a domineering speaker. Conversation is a two-way process. If you just keep on talking, your listener will eventually glaze over, and you will lose that person entirely. Nobody wants to just sit back and listen to someone run his or her mouth; I don't care how interested they are.

- Positive attitude. The attitudes you bring to conversations will have a huge impact on the way you handle yourself and the perceptions of those with whom you are interacting. Choose to be honest, patient, optimistic, respectful, genuine, and accepting, and believe in other people's competence. In other words, no matter how difficult it may be, try to respect what they are saying, even if they themselves don't communicate well. Maybe look a little between the lines of their comments.

- Time and place. Choose the right moment and the right place. If you need to discuss something in private with a person, make sure that the choice of venue is appropriate and that you do not feel uncomfortable about the possibility of being overheard. On the other hand, if you need to make your point before a larger group of people, ensure that the location is somewhere that your discussion will be audible to all who are present, so that you can engage each and every person in conversation.

- Clear and concise. Be clear about the purpose of the communication. For example, your purpose could be to inform others, to obtain information, or to initiate action. You need to know your goals in advance, because each of these objectives requires a different approach. For example, if your intention is to inform without being pedantic, you should be sure that they learn fully what you are teaching. If your purpose is to initiate an action, you must make the best use of rhetoric. Rhetoric is a word that has taken a bad rap lately, but it should be used as a method to persuade others. This can be done in several ways, including demonstrations.

- Organize and clarify ideas. This should be achieved in your mind before you attempt to communicate. If you are passionate about a topic, you may become garbled if you haven't thought of some key points to stick with. A good rule of thumb is to choose three main points prior to speaking and keep your communication focused on those three. That way, if the topic wanders off course, you will be able to return to one (or more) of these three key points without feeling flustered. Which brings us to the next idea…

- Stay on topic. Make sure all facts, stories, allusions, and examples add to the conversation or debate. Again, refer to the three key points. If you have already thought through the issues and the essence of the ideas that you wish to put across to others, it is likely that some pertinent phrases will stick in your mind. Do not be afraid to use these to underline your points—even very confident and well-known speakers have reused their key lines again and again for major effect.

- Practice. Communication skills can be practiced every single day, in settings that range from the social to the more professional. New skills take time to refine, but each time you use your communication skills, you open yourself to new opportunities and future partnerships.

- Be prepared. When you are well prepared, chances of failure and goof-ups are greatly reduced. You feel more relaxed and sure of yourself because you have all your bases covered. You need to know exactly what you are going to talk about. This doesn't mean that you need to memorize exactly what you plan to say. Rather, it means you should have a good outline of relevant facts and information that you can talk about (remember—three key points). Know what you are talking about! It is good to be aware of what type of audience you will be speaking before as well. This will give you an idea of the best approach and tone of your speech. It is also beneficial to check over the conditions under which you will speak. If you can, go up to the podium to check things over and get an overall feel for things. If you will use a microphone, check it out. Even if you're making a presentation in a meeting room at work, it is a good idea to check out the room beforehand and try to visualize how you will be conducting business in that environment.

- Practice more. Even if you know your material very well, practice is extremely important. The more you give a talk, the more automatic it becomes to you. Professional salesmen are taught and encouraged to practice their pitch so much that it truly becomes second nature. That will lessen the chance of faltering, getting lost in your thoughts, or being distracted by a comment that challenges what you are pitching.

> Don't practice till you get it right; practice until you can't get it wrong.
>
> —Unknown

- Have an outline. It is best to have your speech outlined on a few sheets of paper or on 3 × 5 cards. You can then refer to them in case you have a mental lapse. Referring to your notes is certainly acceptable to an audience, so long as you are not reading a speech word for word from a script. Look at public figures who glance down at a card or those whose heads are down all the time; how does this make you feel? You're more likely to trust people who understand exactly what they are trying to say by their eye contact than people who are looking down the entire time reading off a script.

- The audience. The more important the audience or the occasion, the greater your fear can be. You don't want to look like a fool in front of the bosses at work, your peers, or even your friends and relatives. You must realize, though, that the audience is usually on your side. They *want* to hear what you have to say and to see you do well. Before you give your speech, think of them as people who are ready to hear you speak, without reluctance. It is just like talking to your friends.

- Relax. When you are introduced to speak, take three breaths to settle yourself down before you get out of your chair. Then, when you go up to the podium, thank the person who introduced you and count to five before you start speaking. This may seem long, but the point here is to take a second (or five) to chill out. This will allow the audience to get settled and ready to hear you. It also is a way that you can show that you are now in control.

- Summarize. Pull together the most important points and the main point of your message so that you and the speaker recognize what was important during the conversation. Reflecting and sum-marizing are more important for formal and work conversations, but they can help you avoid a lot of relationship conflicts in other areas if practiced properly.

The bottom line is, we hear a lot these days about communication, but far too often we don't have a solid understanding of either how important this is for our success or how to go about it effectively. As we've seen, like anything else worthwhile, it takes some studying, some practice, and a whole lot of common sense. The bottom line is, you need to be very intentional when it comes to communicating well, and never just take it for granted. Be deliberate about how you go about communicating with other people. The positive impression that good communication skills make, and the benefits you will enjoy in your career from how well you express yourself, will no doubt pay dividends for you for years to come, but only if you start making serious efforts on the subject right now.

CHAPTER 10

• • •

TIME MANAGEMENT

LET'S FACE IT. People do not understand the concept of time. You can tell by the way people mope around and move about their lives so slowly. There is no sense of urgency at all, because they think that time is something that is always available. They believe there is a constant supply of it, just like air or water. This is a fallacy; time is not plentiful. People, for the most part, have lost their appreciation for time. These days, it's seen as being infinite. *We don't have all the time in the world!* Most people feel that time is guaranteed, thinking tomorrow will certainly come around after a long night's sleep. *Wrong!* The point that I'm so desperately trying to make throughout this book is that we need to change the way we are living our lives and the priorities by which we live. Time management is something that everyone should appreciate and truly learn to master, because *tomorrow is not guaranteed!*

Many people mistake time *tracking* for time *management.* They religiously keep track of everything they do each day, for weeks or even months, and then they stop doing it because they haven't realized any positive changes. When you think about it, *nothing* can change simply because you know what you are doing at each minute of the day. The point is that you should ask yourself: Is what you are doing the best thing you can be doing to reach your life objective? Thus, solely keeping track of how you spend your time isn't time management. Time management is about *making changes* in the way you spend your time. For effective time management, you must apply a time-management system that will help you see where changes can and should be made. Then you must actually *make the changes.*

Some people have a real knack for planning their time. Many do not. If you are among those who struggle, you may need to take a step toward learning the simple skill of identifying and prioritizing the most important things in your day.

There are three broad categories of how you spend your time: necessity, practicality, and efficiency.

Necessity: These activities are locked in and are nonnegotiable. Examples include child care, customer appointments, meetings, and emergencies. These things are absolute musts in order to simply survive.

Practicality: Practicality involves arranging activities to be accomplished at the best time of day for the specific type of activity. Examples include medical appointments, school activities, volunteerism, time off, vacations, and exercise. So these are also things that you must do, but they can be arranged in a more efficient way.

Efficiency: The best utilization of time and resources is known as efficiency. Efficiency involves wisely delegating, continuously considering improvement and quality, and optimizing teamwork. Some specific aspects of efficient time are listed below.

1. Putting out fires, such as an unexpected urgent phone call, a report that's necessary for a meeting and should have been printed yesterday, or a missing file that should be on your desk. How much of your day was actually spent in crisis mode? For most people, this is a negative category that drains energy and interferes with their productivity.

2. Interruptions. Phone calls and people dropping by your office will probably top the list when you're assigning events to this category. Once again, for most people, this is a negative category because it interferes with (and sometimes kills) productivity.

3. Doing planned tasks. This is the most positive use of time during your workday. During this part, you are in control of your actions and accomplishing what you intended to accomplish. Planned tasks can include phone calls, meetings with staff, and even answering e-mail—so long as these are tasks that you have put on your agenda.

4. Working creatively without interruption. You may not be working on a task you had planned to do, but you are getting around to accomplishing something. For most people, this is a very productive, positive work mode.

5. Uninterrupted downtime. These times are when, during the workday, you reenergize and regroup. Lunch or a midmorning break may count *if* they're uninterrupted. If you're lucky enough to work with a company that offers on-site workout facilities or relaxation rooms, that would count too. Everyone needs a certain amount of uninterrupted downtime built into their day to be productive during their work time.

MAKING THE MOST OF YOUR TIME

1. No matter how organized we are, there are always only going to be twenty-four hours in a day. Time doesn't change. All we can truly manage is ourselves and what we do during the time that we have.

2. Find out where you're wasting time. Many of us fall prey to time wasters that steal time that we could be using much more productively. What are your time bandits? Do you spend too much time Facebooking, tweeting, reading e-mail, making personal calls, or just wasting it away on worthless garbage on the Internet? Track your daily activities so you can form an accurate picture of what you actually do each day. This may be stating the obvious, but I

think you are going to find that there is a big difference between what you think you are accomplishing and what you actually accomplish day in and day out. Try it out!

3. Create time management goals. Remember, the focus of time management is *changing your behaviors*, not changing time. A good place to start is by eliminating your personal time wasters. For one week, for example, set a goal that you're not going to take any personal phone calls while you're working, that you'll do no Facebook at all during the day until you get home from work, or that you'll spend one hour only on your cell phone for the entire day.

4. Implement a time-management plan. The objective is to change your behaviors over time so that you can achieve whatever general goal you've set for yourself, such as increasing your productivity or decreasing your stress. So you need not only set specific goals, but also track them over time to see whether or not you're actually accomplishing them.

5. Use time-management tools. Whether it's a Day-Timer or a software program, the first step to using your time wisely is to know where it's going at the moment and plan how you're going to spend your time better in the future. A software program such as Outlook, for instance, lets you schedule events easily and can be set to remind you of events in advance, making your time-management process even easier. If you don't want to hard schedule your day, at least have a tool to write down or note the things you want to accomplish that day.

6. Prioritize ruthlessly. You should start each day with a time-management session prioritizing the tasks for that day and setting your performance benchmark. If you have twenty tasks for a given day, how many of them do you truly need to accomplish? You need to tackle the hardest one first! My technique is to focus my energy in the morning on the most difficult task. Then,

once I've completed that, I'll drop down and knock out a few lower items to boost my mental state. This makes me feel like I'm really getting shit done because I took care of the most difficult first and then took care of the less important, easier stuff next, but my list *kept getting shorter.* Then I'll go after the next toughest task.

7. Learn to delegate or outsource. No matter how small your business is, there's no need for you to be a one-person show. For effective time management, you need to let other people carry some of the load. This is why it's so important to hire or work with *a solid team!* Trust in them, and you will be just fine.

8. Establish routines and stick to them as much as possible. While crises will arise, you'll be much more productive if you can follow routines most of the time.

9. Get in the habit of setting time limits for tasks. For instance, reading and answering e-mail can consume your whole day if you let it. Instead, set a limit of one hour a day for this task and stick to it.

10. Be sure your systems are organized. Are you wasting a lot of time looking for files on your computer? Take the time to organize a file-management system. Is your filing system slowing you down? Redo it so that it's organized to the point that you can quickly lay your hands on whatever you may need.

11. Don't waste time waiting (I hate waiting!). From client meetings to dentist appointments, it's impossible to avoid waiting for someone or something. But you don't need to just sit there and twiddle your thumbs. Always take something to do with you, such as a report you need to read, a checkbook that needs to be balanced (if you still use them, or online banking), or just a blank pad of paper that you can use to plan your next marketing campaign. Technology makes it easy to work wherever you are; your tablet or cell phone will help you stay connected.

Let us now create a priority chart using some of these concepts, broken down into four main categories:

1. Do now (important/urgent)
   - real major emergencies and crisis issues
   - significant demands for information from superiors or customers
   - project work with imminent deadline
   - meetings and appointments
   - reports and other required submissions
   - staff issues or needs
   - problem resolution, "firefighting," fixes
   - serious urgent complaints

Subject to confirming the importance and the urgency of these tasks, they need to be done now. Prioritize tasks that fall into this category according to their relative urgency. If two or more tasks appear equally urgent, discuss and probe the actual requirements and deadlines with the task originators or with the people dependent on the task outcomes. Help the originators of these demands reassess the actual urgency and priority of these tasks. These tasks should include activities that you'll previously have planned in box 2, which will then move into box 1 when the time slot arrives. If helpful, you should show your schedule to task originators to demonstrate and affirm that you are prioritizing in a logical way, and to be as productive and effective as possible. Look for ways to break a task up into two stages. If it's an unplanned demand, often a suitable initial "holding" response or acknowledgment with a commitment to resolve or complete it at a later date. This will enable you to resume other planned tasks.

Time is what we want most but spend worst.

—WILLIAM PENN

2. Plan to do (important/not urgent)
   - planning and preparation
   - project planning and scheduling
   - research and investigation
   - networking and relationship building
   - thinking and creating
   - modeling, designing, testing
   - systems and process development
   - anticipative, preventative activities or communication
   - identifying need for change and new direction
   - developing strategies

These tasks are most critical to success, and yet they are commonly the most neglected. These activities include planning, strategic thinking, deciding direction and aims, and so on, all crucial for success and development. You must plan time slots for doing these tasks, and if necessary, plan where you will do them free from interruptions. Otherwise, other "urgent" matters will take precedent. Work from home if your normal place of work cannot provide you with a quiet situation and protection from interruption. Break big tasks down into separate, logical stages and plan time slots for each stage. Use project-management tools and methods. Inform other people of your planned time slots and schedules; having a visible schedule is the key to being able to protect and utilize these vital time slots.

3. Reject and explain (not important/ urgent)
   - trivial and "offloaded" requests from others
   - apparent emergencies
   - ad-hoc interruptions
   - misunderstandings appearing as complaints
   - irrelevant distractions
   - pointless routines or activities

- dealing with accumulated unresolved trivia
- duplicated effort
- unnecessary double-checking
- boss's whims or tantrums

Scrutinize these demands ruthlessly, and help originators—even your boss and senior managers—reassess the true importance of these tasks. Practice and develop your ability to explain and justify to them why you do not prioritize these tasks. At first, your superiors may simply view it as task shirking, but a real and honest evaluation can make them see the importance and value of your ideas. After all, it is ultimately for the benefit of everyone involved.

Wherever possible, reject and avoid tasks in this category immediately, informing and managing people's expectations and sensitivities accordingly. Explain why you cannot do these tasks and help the originators find another way of achieving what they need to be accomplished. This might involve delegating to another person or reshaping the demand to be more strategic in order to produce a more feasible solution.

Look for causes of repetitive demands in this area and seek to prevent their recurrence. Educate and train others, including customers, suppliers, fellow staff, and superiors, to identify long-term remedies, not just quick fixes. For significant repetitive demands in this area, create a project to resolve the cause. Challenge habitual systems, processes, procedures, and expectations (e.g., "We've always done it this way"). Help others manage their own time and priorities, so that they don't bounce their pressures onto you. Question old policies and assumptions to see if they are still appropriate.

Lost time is never found.

—Benjamin Franklin

4. Resist and cease (not important / not urgent)
    - unnecessary and unchallenged routines
    - "comfort" activities; computer games, social media, excessive cigarette breaks
    - chat and gossip (face-to-face and over the phone)
    - social and domestic communications
    - junk e-mails and text messages
    - daydreaming
    - interrupting others
    - reading irrelevant material
    - unnecessary adjustments; updating equipment, systems, and screensavers
    - lengthy breaks, frequent canteen or kitchen visits
    - embellishment and overproduction
    - passive world-watching, TV, and so on
    - alcohol and drug abuse
    - aimless travel and driving
    - shopping or buying for no purpose

These activities are not tasks; they are habitual comforts that provide a refuge from the effort required to have discipline and be proactive. These activities affirm the same comfort-seeking tendencies in other people; a group or whole department all doing a lot of this activity creates an unproductive and ineffective organizational culture.

These activities have no positive outcomes and are therefore demotivating. Often, they are stress-related, so consider why you do these things, and if there's a deeper root cause, address it!

The best method for ceasing these activities and for removing temptation to gravitate back toward them is to create a clear structure or a schedule of tasks for each day.

Guide to completing the table:

	Urgent	Not urgent
Important	1. Do *now*	2. Plan to do
Not important	3. Reject and explain	4. Resist and cease

Convince yourself that learning and mastering these techniques will enhance your productivity so much that you can't afford not to do it.

CHAPTER 11

• • •

HEALTH

Physical fitness is not only the key to a healthy body but
it is the basis of dynamic and creative intellectual activity.

—JOHN F. KENNEDY

Twenty percent of health outcomes are genetically
determined. The other 80 percent are determined by
lifestyle.

—DOC EAL

IF YOU'RE LOOKING for a productive way to use your time, one of the best
things you can do is improve your health habits. Without a strong body,
we cannot have an optimal mind or spirit. We can't be our best if our "machine" is running on improper fuel and has poor upkeep. In other words,
take the time to become the healthiest version of yourself.

We are the most medicated country in the world. As a country, we
must have a healthy populace. Take care of yourself! Watch what you eat.
I know you don't like being overweight, so do something about it.

You must exercise (yeah, it's a real thing!). You must take care of your
body. Also, remember to sleep, rest, and just listen to your body. Maybe
you don't *need* to go out on a Friday night with your friends...maybe
you're actually too tired. Your brain is unable to function without the right
amount of rest and rejuvenation.

The bottom line here is that if you are not healthy, all the great information about living a better, happier, more interesting life is all for naught.

You need to treat your body like a finely tuned machine. A machine needs proper and regular tune-ups. Take, for instance, your car. If you don't change your oil, then the vehicle will eventually break down on you, and you'll soon be taking the bus! In the very same way, if you do not eat appropriately and fuel your brain, then you won't be firing on all cylinders. Same thing goes with the physical aspect of your body. If you're not active and getting your body into motion, it remains stagnant and will deteriorate. Take the car example again; if you let your car sit for too long, the tires start to dry rot, and things begin to fall apart. Before you know it, the next time you try to drive that vehicle, it has some serious issues.

Eat healthy, eat nutritious foods, and get outside and get your heart rate up! These are just two good habits that you should adopt immediately. Eating healthy and staying in shape are not just for that New Year's resolution; these are lifelong changes that you need to start and maintain *right now*. You'll most certainly regret it later if you don't.

There are many books that link health, fitness, and nutrition to being successful, motivated, and energetic enough to conquer your biggest obstacles and live out your dreams. Always remember that the fine machine of your body needs maintenance. If you eat right first, you will have the energy and drive to work out, and working out makes you feel good, and when you feel good, you can be productive with your time. There are no shortcuts, and there sure isn't any room for excuses when it comes to your health.

Fitness is an important part of maintaining a healthy life. By making some change in your lifestyle and eating habits, you can move toward a fitter and, in turn, happier life. Moreover, it can be said that fitness correlates directly with our health. If we are not taking care of our bodies, we get sick. You can become fit by following some basic exercises and eating a healthy diet. Good health combined with happiness helps us achieve a higher quality of life.

HEALTH

Part of being fit and healthy is what you eat and how much of it you consume. The macronutrients in food provide you energy, as well as the raw materials your body needs to stay alive. The three macronutrients are fats, proteins, and carbohydrates. If your diet generally follows the USDA Food Guide Pyramid, you are ensured to get the recommended daily allowances of vitamins (the amount people generally need), but there are many reasons why these guidelines might not get us the vitamins we need.

Vitamins are sometimes called micronutrients. Micronutrients do not provide energy for the body, but they are necessary to carry out most biochemical processes. A healthy diet can provide all the vitamins and minerals you need, yet there are times when dietary supplements are important too. Small doses can keep us healthy. However, they are not a substitute for the food that your body needs to make energy and rebuild damaged tissue. Diets that severely restrict or eliminate proteins, fats, or carbohydrates can impair bodily functions, and vitamins cannot make up for that.

Vitamins are not food. But like anything else, vitamins are an important *part* of a healthy diet. Unlike carbohydrates, proteins, and fats, vitamins do not directly provide building blocks or energy for your body; vitamins function as assistants to your body in creating and breaking down building blocks to store and release energy.

You can look at WebMD's page on vitamin and mineral intake or search online for vitamin and mineral intake. This information gives you an idea of the vitamins and minerals needed by the body and in what quantity. You can overdose on vitamins, so be careful. In the rush of daily life, it may be hard to eat a balanced diet. Sometimes we skip meals or buy them from sources (like fast-food restaurants) where we do not have easy access to information about the nutritional value. So taking a multivitamin is sometimes a good idea. I have outlined some other simple guidelines below.

Eat small meals throughout the day rather than big meals and always eat your breakfast, as it helps speed your metabolism, leading to better weight control and proper digestion. Healthy eating means choosing foods that are good for you, using the best cooking methods, and learning portion control.

A good place to start is to learn which foods are healthy and serve your body well. The foods you eat can be divided into different groups to make planning a healthy diet easier. Learn about the food groups via the USDA Food Pyramid. Also, learn the eight-minute rule—that's the amount of time it takes for the brain to register that you are full, so eat slowly and wait for eight minutes to pass before you take a second helping.

Moderate exercise has also been credited for fighting off various illnesses and infections by giving the body a boost in the production of immune cells that attack bacteria. After various studies, it has been discovered that moderate exercise also lowers the risk of cold and flu. Maintaining yourself as fit, or simply getting fit, doesn't necessarily mean attending a gym or working out in an aerobics studio. Choose an activity that you enjoy and you are much more likely to continue with, and notice improvements in yourself. The easiest exercise that you can start with is walking every day. It involves the entire body, and you do not need any special equipment to walk. You can just do it. When you are ready to step up your game, I've included some starting guidelines below.

First, you need to warm up. Doing five to ten minutes of cardio will get your heart rate up and start warming your joints and ligaments. This can be done by running in place or going for a short jog. For a lower-impact warm-up, try doing alternating knee raises or leg kicks. An optimal way to structure your exercise is to do two or three sets of each activity (for example, weight lifting) with twelve to fifteen reps of each exercise.

Many experts have made their living off a set workout routine or program. I want to keep things basic. Remember, you do not need a gym membership to be healthy. You can do air squats to build up your leg and butt muscles. We all know push-ups, which will work your chest and arms. Sit-ups are also something that people can do in their living room to work off that gut most folks have. The point is to get started with something to keep your body and heart healthy. Once you've let your muscles go, you may not be able to bounce back into exercise like you could when you were younger. It can take time to get back into shape. A good rule of thumb is that any regular (e.g., five days per week) exercise program takes three months to show visible results. Hang in there.

> Life expectancy would grow by leaps and bounds if
> green vegetables smelled like bacon.

—Doug Larson

This is all good advice to follow, but one important fact should not be overlooked: you must see your doctor on a regular basis once you turn thirty-five. While this may not be something you want to do, it is quite necessary. Only a blood test is going to tell a detailed story of your body chemistry. Are you deficient in this area or that? Are you developing a disease? Cholesterol problems, maybe? Diabetes? Whatever it may be, the physical exam can reveal problems in time for you to realize them and usually reverse them. The best example is, unfortunately, cancer. The most active, healthy-eating person in the world can contract cancer. There are often no symptoms. The key to preventing cancer is doing all you can to follow a healthy diet and exercise regime. Above and beyond that, routine medical screening beginning at age thirty-five in accordance with the US Preventative Services Task Force guidelines is your best bet. All US physicians are educated to follow these recommendations, which are based on real evidence of benefit. Pop culture teaches us to stay away from doctors and hospitals. While there may be beneficial reasons not to overutilize the medical system, it is always better to deal with an identified problem proactively than to ignore a possible condition you don't even know is shortening your life.

> The two most important things you can do to ensure a
> healthy and long life are not to smoke, and to get regular
> exercise.

—Doctor EAL

CHAPTER 12

• • •

PLANNING FOR LIFE

MUCH IS WRITTEN about growing up and becoming an adult, but there is not much on what happens during those many years of adolescent adulthood. Two of the most important aspects of your life begin when you leave school—careers and relationships. During the adult years, you must set certain goals and achieve them to reach the levels of success that may be part of your dream. You cannot just let fate take its course and drag you along with it. Certain circumstances can hamper your progress, but this is part of the growth and development required in adulthood. Just never stop following your vision.

Very broadly, your goals should align with what I see as the four phases of adulthood:

The "You Don't Know Squat Phase"—approximately 18 to 25 years old: This is when you think you know everything and really screw it up. Most people will buy the car that is outside their budget and most likely get into an accident. Another observation (maybe from experience) is you most likely are drinking too much alcohol and spending way too much money on the weekends. Another thing I've noticed is that during this phase, people can sleep for ten hours and wake up exhausted. I ask myself, how is this even possible? There are so many other pitfalls that can be listed, but that's okay. This is the time to get it all out of your system.

The "Growth Phase"—approximately 25 to 35 years old: This is when you select and establish your career, when you learn and become proficient at what you do. An observation has been made that it generally takes ten years to become really good at what you do; more or less "an expert" in the practice. So, in the first ten years of your adult life, in the "growth phase," you work hard at your career, grow your financial base, buy your first house, find a committed relationship, and settle into adult life.

The "Money Making Years"- approximately 35 to 50 years old: This is when you start taking on leading positions in your job, educate your children, possibly upgrade to a house that you can live in until retirement, and perhaps get the car you always wanted. This is, of course, assuming that you have set your goals and keep working toward them. Making this sort of progress at this particular time is critical. It is very hard to wake up at fifty and decide you now want to become that huge success as you look around and see what others have already done in their lives. In this phase, you either run with the pack or fall behind.

The "Coast Phase"—approximately 50 to retirement age: This is when you need to enjoy your achievements and rise to the expert level in your job. You should now be the successful business owner, the CEO of the company, or one of the senior managers. You take the vacations you've dreamed of and put the kids through college. You get recognition for your achievements and begin to educate the next generation in turn.

The "Retirement Phase"—this is when you can pursue those interests that have always taken a backseat to your career and begin to do more philanthropic work. This may be a holding pattern, where you don't look at starting on new financial projects, but maintain what you presently have. Some people are energetic and healthy enough to create the projects and adventures they didn't have time for previously. Eventually, you may be looking at scaling down the house you live in and possibly traveling the world.

For every one hundred adults, you will have ten achievers and only one success story. It is not easy, but it can be done!

Goal setting is a powerful process for thinking about your ideal future and for motivating yourself to turn this vision into reality.

The process of setting goals helps you choose where you want to go in life. By knowing precisely what you want to achieve, you know where you need to concentrate your efforts in order to do so. Goal setting is an important method for:

- Deciding what is important for you and what you aim to achieve in life
- Separating what is important from what is irrelevant, or simply a distraction
- Motivating yourself
- Building your self-confidence based on successful achievement of goals

Goal-setting techniques are used by top-level athletes, successful businesspeople, and high achievers in all fields. They live on examples of long-term vision and short-term motivation. They focus on acquisition of knowledge and organize their time and resources to make the very most of life. We live in a life of "out of sight, out of mind" mentality. *Get out of it!* Take a tip from the successful people in your life and actively seek mentoring from those people.

The first step in setting personal goals is to consider what you want to achieve in your lifetime (or by a time at least, say, ten years in the future), as setting lifetime goals gives you the overall perspective that shapes all other aspects of your decision-making process. For a broad, balanced coverage of all important areas in your life, try to set goals in some of these categories:

Career: What level do you want to reach in your career?
Physical: Are there any specific athletic goals you want to achieve? What are you going to do to achieve this?
Public Service: Do you want to make the world a better place? If so, how?
Attitude: Is there any part of the way that you behave that upsets you? If so, set a goal to improve your behavior and find a solution to the problem.

Education: Is there any knowledge in particular you want to acquire? What information and skills will you need to achieve other goals?

Family: Do you want to be a parent? If so, how are you going to be a good parent and set your child up for success? *Remember, your kids will emulate you!*

Pleasure: How do you want to enjoy yourself? You should ensure that some of your life is for you and you alone!

Financial: How much do you want to earn, and by what stage of life?

Think about your answers long and hard...and write them down! Everything always seems more serious—and therefore you are more likely to follow through on it—if you put things down in writing. Most importantly, be true to yourself! Don't let others decide your goals for you.

I'm not saying you need to make lifetime goals, but I'm telling you that having goals in mind will give you a path that will lead to a better life you never thought you could achieve. Set a ten-year plan of where you want to live, the job you want to have, and the education you want to achieve. Then set a five-year plan, a one-year plan, a six-month plan, and a one-month plan of progressively smaller goals. Each of these should be based on the previous plan. Then create a daily to-do list of things that you can do today to work toward your lifetime goals. Periodically review the longer-term plans, and modify them to reflect your changing priorities and experiences.

Okay, I know life happens. Someone said, "Life is what happens while you're busy planning other things," and with social media and other electronic platforms, there will have been ten new trends or fads that you have gone through since picking up this book, but the moral to all this is really asking yourself what you want to do with the limited time you have here. It's okay to change your list every year, but just understand one thing: you're not getting any younger. You will have less energy tomorrow than you have today, and someone is working just as hard as you, if not harder, to get to their own goals. *This should really make you think.* No more YOLOD (You Only Live Once, Dummy) attitude. Instead, follow the SMART method and achieve greatness in your life!

SMART MODEL
In the nineteenth century, Elbert Hubbard, an American philosopher, recognized that people had a hard time achieving their goals. So Hubbard came up with the SMART goal system. Pay attention to this acronym and what each letter stands for; it has worked for hundreds of years.

SPECIFIC
Goals should be straightforward and emphasize what you want to happen. Specifics help us focus our efforts and clearly define what we are going to do.

Specific involves the what, why, and how of the SMART model:

What are you going to do? Use action words such as direct, organize, coordinate, lead, develop, plan, and build.
Why is it important to do this at this time? What do you want to ultimately accomplish?
How are you going to do it (and by when)?

Ensure that the goals you set are very specific, clear, and easy to follow. Instead of setting a goal to lose weight or be healthier, set a specific goal to lose two inches off your waistline or to run or walk five miles at a challenging pace.

MEASURABLE
If you can't measure it, you can't manage it. In the broadest sense, the whole goal statement is a measure for the project; if the goal is

accomplished, that is a success. However, there are usually several short-term or small measurements that can be built into the goal.

Choose a goal with *measurable* progress, so you can see the change occur. How will you see yourself when you reach your goal? Be specific! "I want to read three books of at least one hundred pages before the New Year" shows the specific target to be measured. "I want to be a good reader" is not as measurable. This part must be *quantifiable*!

Establish concrete criteria for measuring progress toward the attainment of each goal you set. When you measure your progress, you stay on track, reach your target dates, and experience the exhilaration of achievement that spurs you on to the continued effort required to reach your goals.

ATTAINABLE

When you identify the goals that are most important to you, you begin to figure out ways you can make them come true. You develop the attitudes, abilities, skills, and financial capacity to reach them. You begin seeing previously overlooked opportunities to bring yourself closer to the achievement of your goals.

If, however, you set goals that are too far out of your reach, you probably won't commit to doing what is required to reach them. Although you may start with the best of intentions, the knowledge that it's too much for you means that your subconscious will stop you from ever giving it your best.

A goal needs to stretch you slightly so you feel challenged but confident that you can do it, and it will need a real commitment. For instance, if you aim to lose twenty pounds in one week, we all know that isn't achievable while being healthy (even though I've known *many* people who have attempted to do this). But setting a goal to lose three pounds, and, when you've achieved that, aiming to lose a further three pounds, will keep it achievable for you.

This feeling of success will help you remain motivated and continue setting goals for yourself.

REALISTIC

This is not a synonym for "easy." Realistic, in this case, means "doable." It means that the learning curve is not a vertical slope, that the skills needed to do the work are available, and that the project fits with the overall strategy and goals of the organization. A realistic project may push the skills and knowledge of the people working on it to the limits, but it shouldn't break them.

Devise a plan, or a way of getting there, that makes the goal realistic. The goal needs to be realistic for you and, more specifically, for where you are now. A goal of never again eating sweets, cakes, chips, and chocolate may not be realistic for someone who really enjoys these foods.

For instance, it may be more realistic to set a goal of eating a piece of fruit each day instead of one sweet item. You can then choose to work toward reducing the amount of sweet products gradually when this begins to feel more realistic for you.

Be sure to set goals that you can attain with some effort! Make them too difficult, and you set the stage for failure. Setting them too low sends you the message that you aren't really capable of much. Set the bar high enough for a satisfying achievement!

TIMELY

Set a time frame for the goal: for next week, in three months, by senior year, or two years from today. Putting an end point on your goal gives you a clear target to work toward.

If you don't set a time, the commitment is too vague. It tends not to happen, because you feel you can start at any time. Without a time limit, there's no urgency to start taking action now.

Time must be measurable, attainable, and realistic.

Now you know the basics of goal setting. So what happens if you don't hit your goals? Just quit, give up, and drink your face off? Well, at this point it's in your own hands. You should be able to find the self-motivation to reset, reevaluate, and rewrite your goals. Take the lessons you've un-doubtedly learned from your experiences and set some new goals! This is not a one-and-done type of scenario; this is a continuous situation where you keep growing, keep progressing, keep working, keep pushing, and continue to be a model for others! The easy road is to quit, so what are you going to do?

CHAPTER 13

• • •

NOW IT'S UP TO YOU

CONGRATS. YOU'VE FINISHED my book. I know that you can see now that I am not an author who is full of BS serving up warmed-over clichés with no practical, real-world value. My hope is that what I have taught you will not only take you off the slippery slope that leads to a mediocre life but also put you on the road to making your dreams in life come true.

No matter what your current circumstances, the ability to turn it all around is already in your hands. Success will come to those who truly desire it. Of course, that means having the common sense to use the brains you were born with in the first place. Focus on this new passion. Obstacles are nothing but challenges that you can and will overcome.

For starters, you learned that you are not stuck. That false belief is the biggest stumbling block for the majority of people, the most common excuse for apathy, and the perennial (albeit lame!) explanation for all your past failures. The truth is, you are not stuck but have complete control—not only of your life, but more importantly, of your future.

We also talked about another key element of success: if you do not learn the concept of the dollar and stop making decisions that will anchor you financially, then you may not be able to go after your dream when you've finally figured it out. Notice, however, that I didn't say to stop spending money on things you truly need. In fact, those are the areas where you will get the most bang for your buck. I'm not worried about the money that you're tracking (car payment, rent, cell phone); I'm worried about the money that sifts through your hands without a trace. Understand the concept of a dollar and how the money works.

Another major takeaway from this book should be the importance of good habits. I realize that habits may seem like trivial stuff, but taken collectively, eliminating the bad ones and developing the good ones can literally change your life, both personally and financially. You break a bad habit by replacing it with a good habit.

Strive for more wisdom, knowledge, and experience. Don't be ordinary. And don't be stupid by wasting the precious time that you are given. If you start making the right decisions when you are young, you will avoid years of pain, failure, and defeat down the road. You will end up in a good place at a younger age more prepared to implement your dream.

Life is short, and our wants sometimes get the best of us. Just remember, nobody is forcing you to buy those cars or forcing you to live outside your means…it's *you* making these choices. Find what burns inside you; find out what causes you to get up before your alarm every day; find out what you want to do with the rest of your life. None of the results are a promise that I can make to you. Better than that, the results come from a sacred vow to yourself that only you can make and only you can fulfill.

I've written so many things in this book that I want you to know from my lessons of life. I've said, "What I want you to take away," or "The moral to the story," or "This most importantly." For this book, I want you to know that in this life you will meet many "ordinary" people, people who are part of the crowd. Many people just meander through life, never really feeling inspired or moved to *be something more*. Then there are "extraordinary" people whom you look at or talk to, and you can tell that they are different. When you meet these people, you feel something. This feeling is almost shocking, or it even makes you speechless. There are a lot of ordinary people in this life we live. Don't be ordinary. I want you to be extraordinary. I choose to keep pushing, giving more, giving extra. I choose to be extraordinary. So what are you going to do?

"Two greatest days of your life: The day you were born, and the day you find out why!"

The more specific you are with your answers, the easier it will be to find what you are destined to do!

What do you LOVE to do?	What are you GREAT at?	What type of industry do you see between what you LOVE and what you're GREAT at...? (THAT'S THE INDUSTRY)
•	•	•

ABOUT THE AUTHOR

TYLER A. PENCEK first began making money at the age of three by selling golf balls in his family's backyard. He bought his first house at the age of eighteen. He received a degree in business from Northern Arizona University and earned an MBA by age twenty-one. But then he left the business world to pursue his dream of becoming a pilot in the United States Marine Corps. Now he is committed to making people aware of the real-life lessons that are not taught in school. You can learn more about his program at RealLifeSchool.com.